English Made Simple Ages 11–14

Revision & Practice

KS3 Years 7–9

theme

verb

Master English topics with ease

SCHOLASTIC

Published in the UK by Scholastic, 2023

Scholastic Distribution Centre, Bosworth Avenue, Tournament Fields, Warwick, CV34 6UQ

Scholastic Ireland, 89E Lagan Road, Dublin Industrial Estate, Glasnevin, Dublin, D11 HP5F

SCHOLASTIC and associated logos are trademarks and/or registered trademarks of Scholastic Inc.

© 2023, Scholastic
1 2 3 4 5 6 7 8 9   3 4 5 6 7 8 9 0 1 2

A catalogue record for this book is available from the British Library.

ISBN 978-0702-32679-0
Printed and bound by Bell & Bain Ltd, Glasgow

The book is made of materials from well-managed, FSC-certified forests and other controlled sources.

MIX
Paper from responsible sources
FSC® C007785
www.fsc.org

Author

Cindy Torn

Editorial team

Rachel Morgan, Vicki Yates, Tracey Cowell, Kate Baxter and Laura Stannard

Design team

Dipa Mistry and Jayne Rawlings, Oxford RAW Design

Photographs

page 5: whisking, Ahanov Michael/Shutterstock; page 5: webpage, Studio-pro/iStock; page 6: inscription, Tony Baggett/Shutterstock; page 12: clapperboard and popcorn, 279 Photo Studio/Shutterstock; page 14: stormy sky, Triff/Shutterstock; page 18: whale, Alex Cimbal/Shutterstock; page 26: stingray, Paii VeGa/Shutterstock; page 31: chimneys, vladimir salman/Shutterstock; page 36: dog, SEESAW Graphics/Shutterstock; page 37: bunting, vkulieva/iStock; page 38: seagrass, Damsea/Shutterstock; page 39: merlin, Phoo Chan/Shutterstock; page 42: dog and vegetables, MPH Photos/Shutterstock; page 44: Greta Thunberg, Anders Hellberg/Wikimedia Commons; page 52: forest, Smileus/Shutterstock; page 58: beach, diy13/Shutterstock; page 59: market scene, Nicole Kwiatkowski/Shutterstock

Illustrations

page 10: picnic hamper, David Rojas Márquez; page 15: three witches, Paul Crompton; page 22: Dr Jekyll/Mr Hyde, Jim Eldridge/Oxford Designers & Illustrators; page 32: boy digging, David Rojas Márquez; page 46: Scrooge, Jim Eldridge/Oxford Designers & Illustrators; page 72: monkey paw, David Rojas Márquez

Acknowledgements

The publishers gratefully acknowledge permission to reproduce the following material: pages 8–9: How positive emotions help us, KidsHealth.org from Nemours Children's Health. © 1995–2021. The Nemours Foundation/KidsHealth®; pages 12–13: Ian Freer for the use of a review of *Avatar: The Way of the Water* from Letterboxd.com; page 16: Extract from *Silence is not an Option* by Stuart Lawrence. Text © Stuart Lawrence, 2021. Cover lettering © Justin Poulter, 2022. Cover photo © Tamara Kwan of TammyLynn.co.uk, 2021; page 18: Icelandair, Special Tours; page 20: The Girl of Ink and Stars text © Kiran Millwood Hargrave 2016. Cover Chicken House 2016, designed by Helen Crawford-White. Reproduced with permission of Chicken House Ltd. All rights reserved; pages 26-27: Stingray article, The *Guardian*; page 30: Wild camping article, The *Guardian*; pages 32–33: Extract from *Holes* by Louis Sachar. © Louis Sachar, 1998, Bloomsbury Publishing Plc; page 36: *Yachting World* for the extract from yachtingworld.com; pages 38–39: © Sophie Pavelle, 2022, *Forget Me Not*, Bloomsbury Wildlife UK, an imprint of Bloomsbury Publishing Plc; page 42: Can dogs be vegan?, My Family Vets website; page 44: *No one Is Too Small to Make a Difference* by Greta Thunberg, Penguin Classics. Copyright © Greta Thunberg, 2019, 2021. Reprinted by permission of Penguin Books Limited.

Contents

How to Use the Book

This book has been written to help support English at Key Stage 3. The book will help you recap things you should have learned previously and build on that with new subject information, followed by a chance to practise using this knowledge.

The seven sections in this book break the subject down into different areas so you can choose which topic you want to practise. At the end of the book a progress tracker has been provided so you can see what you have done and what you haven't.

Answers can be found on pages 88–93.

Section

Chapter title

Key Words: these are highlighted within the text and definitions can be found in the glossary (pages 86–87).

Recap: background knoweldge for the topic area

Revise: the information you need to know to answer questions on this topic

Tips: yellow boxes provide you with hints to aid understanding

Check: practice questions to check your understanding from the Revise section. You should write in the book.

Retrieving Information

↺ Recap

Information retrieval means that you find specific information in a text.

📋 Revise

The text below is from a recipe for cupcakes. If you were making these cupcakes, you would need to read the whole recipe. However, before you decide to make them, you might want to **scan** the text to check certain processes and see what the ingredients are.

STEP 2

Using an electric whisk beat 110g softened butter and 110g golden caster sugar together until pale and fluffy then whisk in 2 large eggs, one at a time, mixing well after each addition.

How long should I beat the butter and sugar together? 'until pale and fluffy'

To scan the text, you need to look for key words or phrases that will help you to answer the question.

✔ Check

Read Steps 3 and 4 from the recipe.

Find information from Steps 3 and 4 to answer the questions.

1. How much salt is needed? _____

2. How long should you whisk the mixture after you have added the flour? _____

3. How long do the cakes take to cook?

_____

4. How will you know when the cakes are cooked?

_____

_____

5. If you were following Steps 2–4, what baking equipment would you need?

_____

_____

STEP 3

Add ½ tsp vanilla extract, 110g self-raising flour and a pinch of salt, whisk until just combined then divide the batter between the cupcake cases.

STEP 4

Bake for 15 mins until golden brown and until a skewer inserted into the middle of each cake comes out clean. Transfer to a wire rack and leave to cool completely.

Understanding the Purpose of a Fiction Text

Key Words
character
purpose

↻ Recap

Authors write fiction texts for a number of reasons. For example, to entertain and describe, to inform, instruct and persuade. Writers sometimes include a 'message' behind their story; many novels and stories are written to teach us about life and to question our behaviour, as well as to entertain.

Revise

In *A Christmas Carol*, Charles Dickens wanted to highlight the gap between the rich and the poor in Victorian England. There was a growing view that rich people should do more to help the poor.

In this scene, two charity collectors have arrived at Scrooge's place of business. They have asked him to make a donation to the poor.

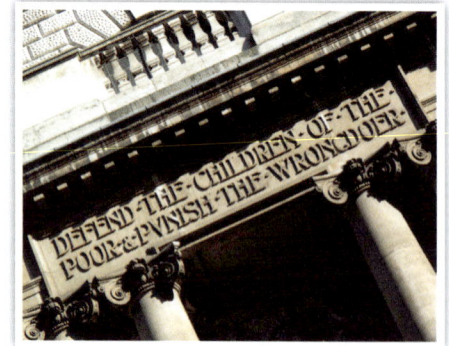

> Prisons were used for criminal offences as well as for people who were unable to pay their debts.

"Are there no prisons?" asked Scrooge.

"Plenty of prisons," said the gentleman, laying down the pen again.

"And the union workhouses?" demanded Scrooge. "Are they still in operation?"

"They are. Still," returned the gentleman, "I wish I could say they were not."

> Workhouses were where prisoners completed cruel and repetitive tasks. The Treadmill was where prisoners ground grain or pumped water for up to eight hours a day. Wages were used to pay off debts.

"The Treadmill and the Poor Law are in full vigour, then?" said Scrooge.

"Both very busy, sir."

"Oh! I was afraid, from what you said at first, that something had occurred to stop them in their useful course," said Scrooge. "I'm very glad to hear it."

> Here, Dickens establishes that Scrooge is a dislikeable **character**.

> The Poor Law established the use of workhouses for people who fell into debt. Dickens campaigned against this law.

To work out a writer's **purpose**, it is helpful to ask yourself questions. For example:

What is the purpose of this text? Why was it written?

Do I agree or disagree with the ideas in the text?

What does the writer want me to think about the ideas or characters in the text?

✔ Check

Aesop's Fables is a collection of fables, or short stories, credited to Aesop, who lived in ancient Greece. Each fable had a moral or message.

Here is an extract from a fable called 'Two Travellers and a Bear'.

> Two men were travelling in company through a forest, when, all at once, a huge bear crashed out of the brush near them.
>
> One of the men, thinking of his own safety, climbed a tree.
>
> The other, unable to fight the savage beast alone, threw himself on the ground and lay still, as if he were dead. He had heard that a bear will not touch a dead body.
>
> It must have been true, for the bear snuffed at the man's head awhile, and then, seeming to be satisfied that he was dead, walked away.
>
> The man in the tree climbed down.
>
> "It looked just as if that bear whispered in your ear," he said. "What did he tell you?"

1. What do you think the bear told the man that was on the ground? Write what you think the bear said.

   _____

   _____

   _____

2. What is the message of this fable? Explain your ideas.

   _____

   _____

   _____

   _____

   _____

Understanding the Purpose of a Non-fiction Text

↺ Recap

Authors write non-fiction texts for a range of reasons. For example, to advise, inform, instruct, explain, persuade and entertain. Often, texts have a mix of purposes (such as instruct and persuade or inform and instruct). To help your understanding, it is useful to recognise the main reason why the writer wrote the text.

🗐 Revise

The text below is from an American health website which looks at the power of positive and negative emotions. Look at how the language helps you to understand the purposes of the text – which are to inform and persuade you to have plenty of positive emotions in your life.

The subheading tells us clearly that this extract will focus on the benefits of positive emotions.

Use of a contrast to show the power of positive emotions over negative emotions.

Use of inclusive language 'our' – we can all benefit.

Use of a three-part list for emphasis.

Inclusive language ('us', 'we'), emphasising the gains we can make.

Directly states the benefits of this approach.

How Positive Emotions Help Us

Positive emotions balance out negative ones, but they have other powerful benefits, too.

Instead of narrowing our focus like negative emotions do, positive emotions affect our brains in ways that *increase* our awareness, attention, and memory. They help us take in more information, hold several ideas in mind at once, and understand how different ideas relate to each other.

When positive emotions open us up to new possibilities, we are more able to learn and build on our skills. That leads to doing better on tasks and tests.

People who have plenty of positive emotions in their everyday lives tend to be happier, healthier, learn better, and get along well with others.

Excerpt from https://kidshealth.org/en/teens/power-positive.html

Lists positive benefits.

✔ Check

Look at this extract from the end of the web page.

1. **Notice and name your positive emotions.** Start by simply focusing on your feelings. You can tune in to your emotions in real time, as they happen. Or take stock at the end of the day, noting how you felt in different situations. For example, you might feel proud when you answer a question right, joyful when your puppy chases you around the yard, or loved when your mom shows up at your game.

   When you first start doing this, you'll probably need to remind yourself to focus on your emotions. But — like any habit — it gets easier the more you do it.

2. **Pick an emotion and act to increase it.** Let's say you choose confidence: What helps you feel confident? How can you get more of that feeling? You might give yourself a "Yes, I can!" pep talk before a test. Or maybe you stand up straighter and practice walking through the halls in a confident way, feeling strong and powerful.

Excerpt from https://kidshealth.org/en/teens/power-positive.html

1. Write down one example where the writer has used a direct statement.

   _____

2. Give one instance where the writer has used an example to demonstrate their point.

   _____
   _____

3. Give one instance where the writer has used a question to demonstrate their idea.

   _____

4. What is the main purpose of this extract? Circle your answer.

   to instruct   to persuade   to entertain

Understanding Fictional Characters

↻ Recap

A character is a person (or sometimes a key figure, such as a creature) in a narrative, play or film.

▤ Revise

In *Three Men in a Boat* (*To Say Nothing of the Dog*) by Jerome K Jerome, three men: George, Harris, Jerome and Montmorency, a fox terrier dog, travel from Kingston upon Thames to Oxford in a boat.

Notice how the men are initially portrayed as sad, but how their mood improves after the 'apple-tart' and becomes even better when they discover the tin of pineapple. Jerome, the narrator, uses a list of three moods to set a humorous tone. This is a clue to show that we should not take these characters too seriously.

We thought of the happy days of childhood, and sighed. We brightened up a bit, however, over the apple-tart, and, when George drew out a tin of pine-apple from the bottom of the hamper, and rolled it into the middle of the boat, we felt that life was worth living after all.

We are very fond of pine-apple, all three of us. We looked at the picture on the tin; we thought of the juice. We smiled at one another, and Harris got a spoon ready.

Here is another list of three actions. Jerome is making fun of the men because a mere tin of pineapple makes them happy.

✓ Check

To fully understand a character, analyse how they speak and behave. Also analyse what other characters say about them.

Read the next part of the text from *Three Men in a Boat* (*To Say Nothing of the Dog*). Then answer the questions below. Note: a 'hitcher' is a boat hook.

> Then we looked for the knife to open the tin with. We turned out everything in the hamper. We turned out the bags. We pulled up the boards at the bottom of the boat. We took everything out on to the bank and shook it. There was no tin-opener to be found.
>
> Then Harris tried to open the tin with a pocket-knife, and broke the knife and cut himself badly; and George tried a pair of scissors, and the scissors flew up, and nearly put his eye out. While they were dressing their wounds, I tried to make a hole in the thing with the spiky end of the hitcher, and the hitcher slipped and jerked me out between the boat and the bank into two feet of muddy water, and the tin rolled over, uninjured, and broke a teacup.
>
> Then we all got mad.

1. The first paragraph is a list of actions. How are the three men behaving?

2. In the second paragraph, what does Harris do and what is the result?

3. In the second paragraph, what does George do and what is the result?

4. In the second paragraph, what does Jerome do and what is the result?

5. Look at the final sentence: 'Then we all got mad'. The writer is making fun of the characters. How do we know this?

Identifying the Main Point in Non-fiction Texts

Key Words
topic sentence
review

↻ Recap

In non-fiction, each paragraph usually has a main point, which is often found in the opening or **topic sentence**.

The main point is often developed by:

- supporting details
- examples
- further information on the topic
- commentary or discussion

📄 Revise

This is an extract from a **review** of the film *Avatar: The Way of Water*.

This is the main point – the topic sentence showing how this film relates to the first, original film.

Avatar: The Way of Water is set some 14 years after the events of the first film. If the original was an inter-species romance, the sequel is a family saga set against the backdrop of the raging guerrilla war between the blue-skinned Na'vi and humans, embodied by the voracious Resources Development Agency (RDA).

Former human soldier Jake Sully (Sam Worthington) and Na'vi warrior Neytiri (Zoe Saldaña) now have four children: Neteyam (Jamie Flatters), Lo'ak (Britain Dalton), Tuktirey, known as Tuk (Trinity Bliss), plus Kiri, the Sully's adopted teenager played in performance capture by Sigourney Weaver (who played scientist Grace Augustine in *Avatar*).

Supporting detail to show the link between the films.

Further information on the topic.

Further information about the cast.

Supporting detail about children to show how time has passed.

Supporting detail to show the link between the films.

Further information about the cast.

Identifying the main point in a paragraph can help you to understand a whole article.

✔ Check

Read this paragraph from the same review and answer the questions below.

As with the first film, Cameron juggles beauty and terror in equal measures. The film is filled with brand new fauna and wildlife, and at the heart of the film is a touching relationship between middle Sully child Lo'ak and a tulkun, a giant whale-like creature, named Payakan. The threat comes in the return of the formidable Colonel Miles Quaritch (Stephen Lang), who was killed by Neytiri in the first film and returns as an autonomous avatar, this time in Na'vi form.

1. What is the main point of this paragraph?

2. Find one example of 'beauty'.

3. Find one example of 'terror'.

4. The writer adds further information with a description of a 'touching relationship'. Describe Payakan.

5. At the end of the review, the writer adds additional information about the making of the film. Highlight the main point in each of these paragraphs.

To perform in the underwater scenes, Cameron brought in world champion freediver Kirk Krack to teach the cast how to do sustained breath holds and still act. The record for the longest breath hold by the actors went to Kate Winslet, who managed seven minutes and 14 seconds.

The performance-capture filming took place in a 900,000-gallon tank (built specifically for the production), which could mimic the ocean's swirling currents and crashing waves. To help acclimatise to the aquatic life, the cast became certified divers and went on a field trip to Hawaii to dive with manta rays.

Understanding Context in Fiction Texts

Key Word

context

↻ Recap

When you read a fiction text, understanding the **context** of the text can help you to unlock its meaning. The context can be historical (when the text was written or set), social (what the text tells you about society or humans in general) or cultural (what the text tells you about a specific culture).

📑 Revise

In Shakespeare's *Macbeth*, Macduff and Lennox have just arrived at Macbeth's castle. Macbeth has murdered King Duncan. Macduff and Lennox do not know this.

What is happening	Extract	Context
Lennox is recounting the strange happenings of the previous evening.	**LENNOX** The night has been unruly. Where we lay,	The murder of a king is called regicide. This was believed to be a terrible sin as people thought that the monarch ruled directly from the will of God. Anyone plotting to kill a king was placing themselves above God.
The weather is strange and stormy. Chimneys have been blown down.	Our chimneys were blown down, and, as they say,	
Death cries and the sounds of people mourning were heard.	Lamentings heard i' the air; strange screams of death,	By killing King Duncan, Macbeth is disrupting the natural order and terrible events will happen.
	And prophesying with accents terrible	
	Of dire combustion and confused events	King James I, who was on the throne when Shakespeare wrote *Macbeth*, had many plots against him and these would be fresh in people's minds – especially the Gunpowder Plot.
	New hatch'd to the woeful time. The obscure bird	
The earth shook like a person with a fever (earthquake).	Clamour'd the livelong night. some say, the earth Was feverous and did shake.	

It is helpful to consider context when you read a text; it can give you new insights to add to your own ideas.

✔ Check

King James I was terrified of witches and believed that a group of witches had plotted against him. James I was also a patron of Shakespeare's theatre company. Shakespeare would have wanted to flatter and agree with the king's views.

Read the extract from the opening scene of *Macbeth* and answer the questions.

A deserted place. *Thunder and lightning*.

Enter THREE WITCHES

First Witch

When shall we three meet again
In thunder, lightning, or in rain?

Second Witch

When the hurlyburly's done,
When the battle's lost and won.

Third Witch

That will be ere the set of sun.

First Witch

Where the place'?

Second Witch
Upon the heath.

Third Witch

There to meet with Macbeth.

---

1. What are the witches planning to do in the opening lines? _____

2. Where do the witches say they will meet Macbeth? _____

3. The third witch predicts the end of the battle. When will this happen? _____

4. This scene with the witches opens the play. Why does Shakespeare do this? Circle your response.

| Shakespeare wanted the audience to be frightened. | Shakespeare wanted to establish that supernatural and evil forces dominate the play. | Shakespeare wanted to attract crowds and people like witches. |

Understanding Context in Non-fiction Texts

↻ Recap

Understanding the context of a non-fiction text can help you to unlock its meaning. Some writers make the context of their writing explicit by explaining why they wished to write the text and what they want the reader to understand.

📄 Revise

In his book, *Silence is Not An Option: Find Your Voice and Be Your Best Self*, Stuart Lawrence talks about what he has learned from life and the tools that have helped him live positively.

In the introduction, Lawrence sets out the context of why he wants to pass on his message.

> Stuart Lawrence establishes the context of the book. This 'major event' changed his life.

In 1993, when I was a teenager, a major event happened in my life. My big brother, Stephen Lawrence, was tragically murdered in a racially motivated attack. For a few readers, this might be the first time you've heard of Stephen. Some of you might have a big brother or sister and know how amazing it is to have one. It's great having someone to look up to, do things with and grow up with. As younger siblings, we often try to copy our big brothers and sisters and try to be as good as them. This was how I was with my brother, Stephen, I admired him like you would admire a superhero.

> The writer explains what happened to his brother.

> The text places this event into the context of every reader's life. The reader understands the impact of this terrible event.

> The text returns to the context of Stuart's own life, showing how much he admired his brother.

When you are trying to understand context in non-fiction texts, ask questions such as:

- Who wrote this text?
- Why did they write it?
- Is it successful in achieving its aims?

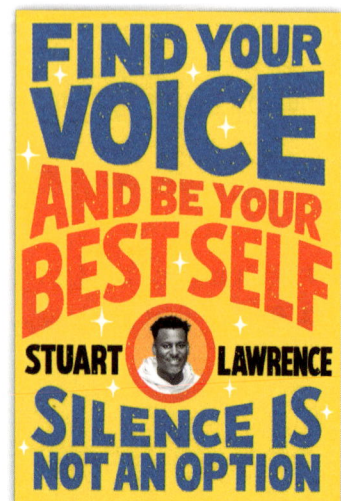

FIND YOUR VOICE AND BE YOUR BEST SELF
STUART LAWRENCE
SILENCE IS NOT AN OPTION

✔ Check

Read the extract from Stuart Lawrence's book and answer the questions.

> Don't you just hate it when you hold the door open for someone and they don't say thank you? As the saying goes, manners cost nothing. In my opinion, manners have helped me more in life than anything else. Good manners make people feel more comfortable around you. You could even say being polite is a superpower!
>
> Beyond being polite, one of the greatest superpowers a person can have is being kind. Even small things, like sharing a smile with someone, offering to help someone with their bags or giving a compliment to someone can go a really long way. These kindnesses can even help to boost other people's self-confidence. What small act of kindness were you once shown that you will never forget? Did it boost your self-confidence?

1. In the first paragraph, what does Stuart Lawrence name as a superpower? _____

2. Find three statements that Lawrence makes about manners.

   _____

   _____

   _____

3. What superpower does Lawrence name in the second paragraph? _____

4. What examples does Lawrence give of small things people can do?

   _____

   _____

   _____

5. Thinking about the context of the book, why do you think Stuart Lawrence wants to pass on these positive messages?

   _____

   _____

   _____

   _____

   _____

Fact or Opinion?

Key Words
fact
opinion

↻ Recap

It's useful to be able to understand whether information in a text is **fact** or **opinion**.

📄 Revise

The text below is from an advert for whale watching tours in Iceland.

This is a fact. It can be proved.

This is an opinion. It cannot be proved.

Whales are currently the largest species on earth, and yet it can be hard to fully comprehend how enormous and boisterous these creatures are when encountering them in their natural habitat.

When you book this tour today with Icelandair Holidays, the opportunity is yours to view these phenomenal creatures up close at the great **Whales of Iceland Exhibition**. This fascinating exhibit, the largest in Europe, displays 23 life-size models of whale species found in the ocean waters around Iceland, along with the history and interesting facts about each. Standing beside these life-size creatures is a unique experience both awe-inspiring, and humbling.

This is a fact.

This is opinion.

This is a fact.

This is opinion.

This is a fact.

The purpose of this text is to persuade you to go on the tour, so it uses a mixture of facts and opinions to influence you.

Statements using opinions like 'awe-inspiring' and 'humbling' are chosen to impact your emotions and persuade you to take part in the experience.

The use of words like 'unique' is interesting – this appears to be a fact but it is an opinion.

Facts can be shown to be true.
Opinions are beliefs that cannot be proved.

✔ Check

Bill Bryson is an American travel writer. In his book *Notes from a Small Island*, he travels around the UK giving his views about the places he visits. In the extract below, he travels to the seaside town of Blackpool.

Read the extract and answer the questions.

> Blackpool – and I don't care how many times you hear this, it never stops being amazing – attracts more visitors every year than Greece and has more holiday beds than the whole of Portugal. It consumes more chips per capita than anywhere else in the planet. (It gets through 40 acres of potatoes a day.) It has the largest concentration of roller-coasters in Europe. It has the continent's second most popular tourist attraction, the 42-acre Pleasure Beach, whose 6.5 million annual visitors are exceeded in number only by those going to the Vatican. It has the most famous illuminations. And on Friday and Saturday nights it has more public toilets than anywhere else in Britain; elsewhere they call them doorways.
>
> Whatever you may think of the place, it does what it does very well – or if not very well at least very successfully.

1. Read the statements below and label them as facts or opinions. The first one has been done for you.

Statement	Fact or opinion?
and I don't care how many times you hear this	opinion
it never stops being amazing	
attracts more visitors every year than Greece	
It gets through 40 acres of potatoes a day.	
It has the largest concentration of rollercoasters in Europe.	
it does what it does very well – or if not very well at least very successfully.	

2. Do you think Bill Bryson likes Blackpool? Refer to his use of facts and opinions in your answer.

_____

_____

_____

_____

_____

Inference 1

↺ Recap

When you read a fiction text, you know details about it because the writer tells you directly or, as a reader, you can **infer** the details. This process of being able to read between the lines is called inference.

📄 Revise

Look at the cover of the novel *The Girl of Ink & Stars* by Kiran Millwood Hargrave. What can you see and what can you infer?

You can infer that in the book there will be links to the natural world.

You can see the central female character: 'The Girl'.

You can infer that the book will include creativity – art or writing.

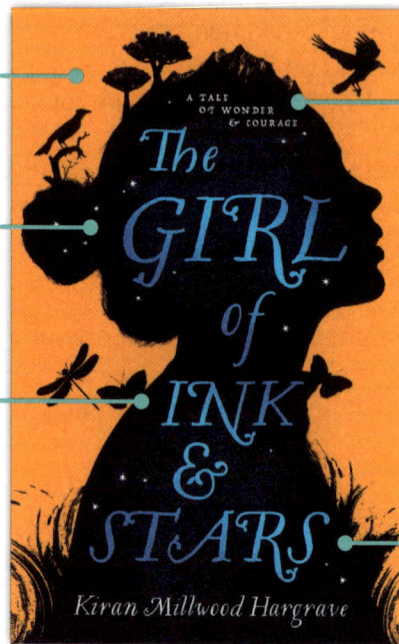

The word 'wonder' suggests that the events in the story will inspire awe in the reader. From the word 'courage', you can infer that the story will feature brave acts.

You can infer that the book might involve adventure; it also suggests a sense of mystery.

A TALE OF WONDER & COURAGE

The GIRL of INK & STARS

Kiran Millwood Hargrave

Now look at this sentence from the opening chapter of the novel. Let's look at what you are told directly and what you can infer.

You are told that something is going to start.

You are told the time of day.

The morning it began was like any other.

You are told that it was a normal day.

You can infer that something unusual (or perhaps even extraordinary) is going to happen. It is an event that 'began' that day, suggesting that it is something that will go on for some time.

The writer contrasts the normal day, 'like any other', with the new events that 'began' that day.

Identify what you are told directly by the writer.

Explore what you can infer by reading between the lines – be a detective!

Consider how direct details and inference builds your understanding of a text.

✔ Check

Look at this extract from the opening chapter of *The Girl of Ink & Stars* and answer the questions.

They say the day the Governor arrived, the ravens did too. All the smaller birds flew backwards into the sea, and that is why there are no songbirds on Joya. Only huge, ragged ravens. I'd watch them perch on the rooftops like omens, and try to squint them into the chaffinches and goldcrests Da drew from memory. If I imagined hard enough, I could almost hear them singing.

"Why did the songbirds leave, Da?" I'd ask.

"Because they could, Isabella."

"And the wolves? The deer?"

Da's face would darken. "Seems the sea was better than what they were running from."

1. What happened to the songbirds? What does this suggest about the arrival of the Governor and ravens?

_____

_____

2. What is an omen? The ravens are described as perching like 'omens' on rooftops. What does this word suggest about the ravens?

_____

_____

3. What happened to the wolves and deer? What does this suggest about the ravens?

_____

_____

4. The Governor is linked to the ravens in the first line. What does this suggest about the Governor's arrival?

_____

5. The writer states that 'Da's face would darken'. What does this suggest about Da's thoughts and feelings?

_____

Inference 2

↺ Recap

When you are introduced to a character, you use inference to work out what type of person they might be. Focus on what you are told directly by the writer and what you can infer from this.

📝 Revise

In Chapter 1 of *The Strange Case of Dr Jekyll and Mr Hyde* by Robert Louis Stevenson, two characters, Enfield and Utterson, are talking about an incident where a man trampled a child in the street. This is our first glimpse of Mr Hyde.

Hyde does not react to his capture, suggesting he is in control of his emotions.

> He was perfectly cool and made no resistance, but gave me one look, so ugly that it brought out the sweat on me like running. The people who had turned out were the girl's own family; and pretty soon, the doctor, for whom she had been sent, put in his appearance. Well, the child was not much the worse, more frightened, according to the Sawbones; and there you might have supposed would be an end to it. But there was one curious circumstance. I had taken a loathing to my gentleman at first sight. So had the child's family, which was only natural. But the doctor's case was what struck me. He was the usual cut and dry apothecary, of no particular age and colour, with a strong Edinburgh accent and about as emotional as a bagpipe. Well, sir, he was like the rest of us; every time he looked at my prisoner, I saw that Sawbones turn sick and white with the desire to kill him.

Even with just a look, Hyde causes a bad reaction in people.

Stevenson begins to suggest that things are not what they might seem.

Enfield, the family and the doctor hate Hyde on sight. This is unusual.

Stevenson adds physical details of how much the doctor hated Hyde.

✔ Check

Read the rest of the extract and answer the questions below.

> I knew what was in his mind, just as he knew what was in mine; and killing being out of the question, we did the next best. We told the man we could and would make such a scandal out of this as should make his name stink from one end of London to the other. If he had any friends or any credit, we undertook that he should lose them. And all the time, as we were pitching it in red hot, we were keeping the women off him as best we could for they were as wild as harpies. I never saw a circle of such hateful faces; and there was the man in the middle, with a kind of black sneering coolness — frightened too, I could see that — but carrying it off, sir, really like Satan. "If you choose to make capital out of this accident," said he, "I am naturally helpless. No gentleman but wishes to avoid a scene," says he. "Name your figure."

1. Enfield said that they could not kill Hyde. What two things do they plan to do instead?

_____

_____

2. How do the people in the crowd react towards Hyde?

_____

_____

3. How does Hyde react to the crowd?

_____

4. Hyde is linked to Satan. Why does Stevenson make this link?

_____

5. Stevenson states that Hyde had a 'sneering coolness'. What does this suggest about his thoughts and feelings?

_____

_____

Inference in Non-fiction

↻ Recap

Use inference to work out what the writer might be telling you between the lines.

📄 Revise

In the text below, the owner of The Cool Cat Café is responding to a review from a customer. Think about what the original review may have said and how the owner feels.

> Acknowledgement of the review.

> The owner feels the criticisms are unproven.

Thank you for taking the time to leave The Cool Cat Café a detailed review. We do appreciate constructive customer feedback as we use it to help us improve. In order to address the concerns in your review, I will examine them point by point. However, I think it is important to state that I think your criticisms are questionable. Nevertheless, the Cool Cat Café will always support your right to voice your opinion.

1) The floors and table surfaces in the café are cleaned regularly in line with national hygiene regulations. As you enter the café, you will see that we hold 5 out of 5 stars for our food hygiene rating. Our vision statement outlines our endeavour to create a 'cool' café where our customers and cats can relax in a safe and clean environment. We are proud of our thorough cleaning processes and we have a dedicated page on our website outlining our cleaning rota and products to reassure customers. The flooring, created by our award-winning design team, adds to the jungle and wildlife theme. It does have dark, grass-like areas that you have mistaken for dirt.

2) I am very sorry that you were served a vegetarian pie rather than a meat one. However, having spoken to staff subsequently I discovered that rather than bringing the matter to our attention calmly, you shouted at our waiting staff, threw the pie on the ground and then refused the meat replacement pie that we offered. I appreciate that the order mix-up should not have happened. However, in a busy café environment, mistakes can happen. We were swift in both our offer of a replacement and an apology from the café manager. I am unsure what else you could have expected from us.

> The café's hygiene and cleaning rota is detailed. This suggests that the review criticised cleanliness.

> This directly states that the reviewer was wrong.

> This suggests that the review criticised the food service.

> List of three actions suggests disapproval of the customer's behaviour.

> Acknowledgement of mistakes made, countered by the compensation that was offered.

Think about the tone of the writing. For instance, is it angry, happy, formal or informal? This will help you to read between the lines.

✔ Check

Read the next section of the owner's response to the review. Then answer the questions.

> 3) In your review, you state that the Cool Cat Café has a distinct lack of cats.
>
> Did you look around the whole café? We have 15 cats to delight and entertain our customers. One of our cats, Wilfred, is a 100 cm from nose to tail Maine Coon. He is a celebrity in this area due to his muscular frame. And because of his size, he is very hard to miss. Our three Siamese cats are admittedly smaller, but they are extremely vocal and amuse our customers with their confident opinions on everything – from their food to who is sitting in their favourite chair.
>
> Our staff members are trained in cat management as well as food services. They support customers with all cat matters, including stroking, brushing and encouraging cats to sit on laps. It is disappointing that you didn't feel able to mention your dissatisfaction regarding this to the staff as we would have been more than happy to show you the cats you appear to have missed.

1. What is this part of the review criticising?

_____

2. What two things does the owner suggest the customer could have done?

_____

_____

3. The owner uses the word 'disappointing' in the final sentence. What does this suggest? Circle your response.

The owner is dissatisfied with the way staff behaved and wants to make amends to the customer.	The owner suggests the customer should have spoken with staff to resolve the situation.	The owner is disappointed that the customer has had a bad experience and wants to put it right.

4. In the final part of the response to the review, the Cool Cat Café owner addresses the customer's accusation that the only cat they saw was a 'flea-bitten moggy'. Write what you think the owner might say.

_____

_____

_____

Inference and the Writer's Intention

↺ Recap

Analysing language choices helps you to work out what the writer wants you to feel about a subject. This is called writer's intention.

🗎 Revise

In an article in the *Guardian* newspaper, Helen Sullivan writes about the nature of a stingray. Think about *what* she tells you and *how* she tells you – by analysing language choices.

The writer tells us that stingrays, like some other creatures, are 'venomous'. However, 'Most' suggests that the stingray is different to other creatures.

Most venomous creatures store their poison in a gland. Not the stingray, whose venom is in its very tissue.

Where do you begin with an animal whose mouth looks like a face, whose face is split into two – half at the top, and half the bottom; who can breathe with either part – from spiracles behind the eyes, or gills behind the mouth; whose teeth are scales; whose scales are teeth-like (denticles)?

The writer uses 'Not' to signal that the stingray is different; the 'venom is in its very tissue' suggests that the whole creature is highly dangerous.

Direct address with a question; this focuses attention on the otherworldly aspects of the stingray.

Features of the stingray are listed but differences between normality and the stingray are emphasised. The mouth 'looks like a face' but that 'face is split into two'. Its breathing, teeth and scales are alien.

What the writer tells you and *how* they tell you give you clues about their intentions and purpose.

✔ Check

In the article from the *Guardian*, the writer's purpose is to inform you about the nature of stingrays. The details she includes help you to look beneath the surface meaning to understand her point of view.

Read the next section of the article, then answer the questions.

When stingrays hunt, they lose sight of their prey – their eyes are bad, and their prey is often underneath them. To find and feel clams, mussels, crabs and fish, the rays rely on electroreceptors in their skin, or, as *National Geographic* puts it, "special gel-filled pits". They literally inhale their food, gulping down the electric signal. As they do this, they breathe through the spiracles behind their eyes, which work less efficiently than their gills. Do they get a little light-headed, breathing as if through a towel, feeling the electricity brighten, speed up, then die?

"Maybe it's like feeling the presence of someone hiding in a dark room," says the narrator of a YouTube video explaining how this electric sense works.

1. Find one piece of evidence to show that the writer thinks the stingray has developed a special ability.

_____

2. Find three pieces of evidence that give a negative impression of the stingray.

_____

_____

_____

3. How do you know that the stingray fascinates the writer?

_____

_____

_____

4. Look at this extract from later in the article. How does the writer want us to feel about the stingray?

Stingrays are venomous. Most venomous creatures store their poison in a gland. Not the stingray, whose venom is in its very tissue. It has no bones. Poisonous tissue, electric senses: where do you begin?

_____

_____

_____

Identifying Themes

Key Word

stanza

↻ Recap

In literature, a writer may explore big ideas that inform us about our own lives or what it is to be human. For example, a novel about going to a new school could be about growing up or could be about facing fears – or both.

📄 Revise

In his poem, 'The Charge of the Light Brigade', Alfred, Lord Tennyson imagines the brigade commander urging his cavalry (soldiers on horseback) to ride through a valley towards enemy guns. The poem tells the story of this event but also teaches us big ideas about war.

Here are the first two **stanzas**.

Heroism The cavalry act without fear or hesitation. They charge towards the guns bravely and heroically.

War The violence and brutality of war is hinted at as they ride into 'the valley of Death'.

Duty The cavalry put duty to their country before their own lives. They follow the order even though this order is wrong: 'Someone had blundered'.

Futility of war These men will not survive this order but they do not question it. They could not 'reason why'.

I

Half a league, half a league,
Half a league onward,
All in the valley of Death
 Rode the six hundred.
 "Forward, the Light Brigade!
 Charge for the guns!" he said.
Into the valley of Death
Rode the six hundred.

II

"Forward, the Light Brigade!"
Was there a man dismayed?
Not though the soldier knew
 Someone had blundered.
 Theirs not to make reply,
 Theirs not to reason why,
 Theirs but to do and die.
Into the valley of Death
Rode the six hundred.

When you are reading literature, think about these questions:

- What's the story about?
- What's the message?
- What do you learn?

✔ Check

1. Draw lines to link each theme with a plot point.

Theme	Plot point
humankind's confrontation with nature	falling in love for the first time
death	moving to university
growing up	someone struggles in a storm at sea
love	a funeral brings a family together
conflict	two friends fight over who was right and who was wrong

2. Write a short plot point for each of these themes.

Friendship _____

Greed _____

Abuse of power _____

Dreams and ambitions _____

Betrayal _____

3. Draw lines to match each novel description with a theme.

Novel description	Theme
Struggles between generations make for a roller coaster of a plot.	growing up
On the shores of a sleepy seaside town, something hideous crawls from the sea.	good versus evil
The village had its own ways of thinking. They had worked – until now.	family conflict
In this rite-of-passage novel, we learn the struggles of realising that parents don't always know best.	change versus tradition

Structuring an Argument

Key Words
argument
structure
emotive language
anecdote

↻ Recap

An **argument** text tries to convince you that the opinion put forward is correct. The writer does this through their ideas and how they **structure** the points – the order they use and their language choices.

📄 Revise

In this article from the *Guardian*, the writer talks about a high court ruling that will stop people wild camping in Dartmoor national park. This ruling will have an impact on school group activities, like the Ten Tors challenge.

The headline sets out the writer's opposition to the camping ban.

The subheading uses **emotive language** such as 'outrage' and 'already banned' to establish the point of view. Use of a statistic to reinforce viewpoint.

Establishing the writer's opinion.

Anecdote to establish why we should agree with the opinion.

Establishing that the writer is not alone in their opinion.

The Dartmoor wild camping ban further limits our right to roam. It must be fought

The high court ruling is an outrage when we are already banned from 92% of the country's land

When I did the Ten Tors challenge at school in 2013, I would fight back tears with my teammates, anticipating the relief and joy we would feel at crossing the finish line after 45 miles of backpacking on Dartmoor. On Friday, different tears fell.

Messages flooded my phone announcing that the right to wild camp on Dartmoor had been overturned in an astonishing defeat.

Use of an **anecdote** – a teenage memory – focusing on emotions: 'tears' and 'joy' following participation in a local challenge. This establishes why the reader should trust the writer's opinion – long-held local knowledge.

The writer is not alone in this opinion. 'Flooded' suggests this is an opinion that is held by lots of others.

Emotive language like 'overturned' and 'astonishing' is used to emphasise the writer's opinion of the court's decision.

Sum up the content of each paragraph of a text to help work out its structure.

✔ Check

The text below is from a campaign group that supports people to make their views known about environmental issues. In this email, the group wants people to sign a petition.

In each row, sum up what the text is saying. Also note any key language features that are being used to persuade you to sign. The first row has been completed to help you.

Dear friends,

Enough is enough!

For decades, **big oil and gas CEOs have misled** the public about the deadly impact of burning fossil fuels that are **cooking our planet**. Now we're seeing murderous floods, deadly droughts and rainforests on fire.

Next week, top CEOs are meeting at a key business summit in the Swiss mountains, pretending they care for the planet — while digging new oil and gas fields, and making billions in profit.

We will travel to Switzerland in the coming days, bringing a **'cease and desist' letter** to oil and gas CEOs, demanding they stop any new oil and gas projects. Join us — **let's have millions of us speaking up** and showing them that we see through their lies. Add your name now!

1. Greeting the reader. 'Friends' suggests we are working together.

2.

3.

4.

5.

Language Choices in Fiction

↺ Recap

A writer creates atmosphere in a text through the language choices they make. This could be by focusing on specific details, varying the length and type of sentences, and through the words they choose.

📑 Revise

This is an extract from Chapter 29 of *Holes* by Louis Sachar. Five boys have escaped from Camp Green Lake, a prison boot camp in a desert in Texas. The boys are called Stanley, X-Ray, Squid, Armpit and Zigzag.

How does Louis Sachar create atmosphere in the opening section of Chapter 29?

> A direct statement that sets the tone. A single-sentence paragraph.

There was a change in the weather.

For the worse.

> Adds information to the previous statement – the situation has changed but it's a bad change. It is not a sentence – it's a **subordinate clause** – so it is incomplete and is used to make the reader feel uncomfortable.

The air became unbearably humid. Stanley was drenched in sweat. Beads of moisture ran down the handle of his shovel. It was almost as if the temperature had gotten so hot that the air itself was sweating.

> This vocabulary signals 'wetness' in some way. This contrasts with the dry and hot desert.

> This vocabulary signals discomfort.

A loud boom of thunder echoed across the empty lake.

> The sense of hearing – 'boom' is **onomatopoeic**. Another change.

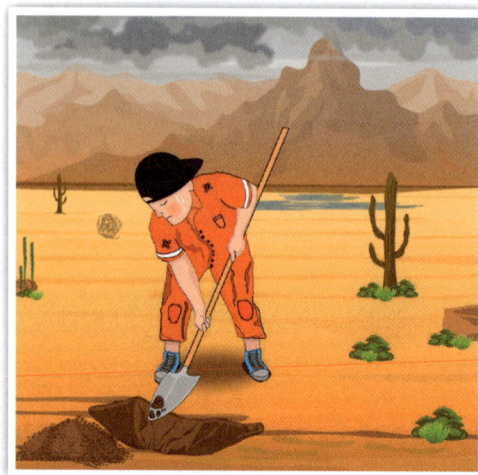

✔ Check

Read the opening section of Chapter 29 from *Holes* and answer the questions.

A storm was way off to the west, beyond the mountains. Stanley could count more than thirty seconds between the flash of lightning and the clap of thunder. That was how far away the storm was. Sound travels a great distance across a barren wasteland.

Usually, Stanley couldn't see the mountains at this time of day. The only time they were visible was just at sunup, before the air became hazy. Now, however, the sky was very dark off to the west, and every time the lightning flashed, the dark shape of the mountains would briefly appear.

"C'mon, rain!" shouted Armpit. "Blow this way!"

"Maybe it'll rain so hard it will fill up the whole lake," said Squid. "We can go swimming."

"Forty days and forty nights," said X-Ray. "Guess we better start building us an ark. Get two of each animal, right?"

"Right," said Zigzag. "Two rattlesnakes. Two scorpions. Two yellow-spotted lizards."

The humidity, or maybe the electricity in the air, had made Zigzag's hair even more wild-looking. His frizzy blonde hair stuck almost straight out.

The horizon lit up with a huge web of lightning. In that split second Stanley thought he saw an unusual rock formation on top of one of the mountain peaks. The peak looked to him exactly like a giant fist, with the thumb sticking straight up.

Then it was gone.

And Stanley wasn't sure whether he'd seen it or not.

---

1. Find and highlight examples of:
   - single-sentence paragraphs
   - contrasting sentence lengths
   - repetition of words or the **rule of three**.

2. Find and highlight three details that show the movement of the storm.

3. Use your highlights and other evidence from the text to explain how Louis Sachar creates atmosphere in the opening section of Chapter 29.

_____

_____

_____

_____

_____

_____

Language Choices in Poetry

↻ Recap

When writers want to explore complex ideas, they often use **figurative language**. You use figurative language to express yourself in everyday speech too. You might describe someone as being 'as red as a beetroot', for example. Figurative language includes the use of **similes**, **metaphors** and onomatopoeia – anything that adds a flourish to writing or speech.

📄 Revise

In his poem 'The Road Not Taken', Robert Frost uses an **extended metaphor** to help the reader understand the journey we take in life and how the choices we make can change that journey.

Here are the first two stanzas of the poem.

The title introduces the idea of the choices we make in life. In this case, the road we didn't take.

The Road Not Taken

Two roads diverged in a yellow wood,
And sorry I could not travel both
And be one traveler, long I stood
And looked down one as far as I could
To where it bent in the undergrowth;

Then took the other, as just as fair,
And having perhaps the better claim,
Because it was grassy and wanted wear;
Though as for that the passing there
Had worn them really about the same,

Robert Frost

Despite feeling sad that both roads can't be taken, a decision needs to made.

The speaker is carefully weighing up the options, trying to make an informed decision.

A decision is made. At first the second path seems to be a better choice.

However, on second thought, it seems that many other people had made the same decision.

Metaphors compare one thing with another. For example: Snow is a white blanket on the ground. Similes also compare two things but use 'like' or 'as'. For example: As white as snow, the petals lay on the ground.

✔ Check

Read the rest of 'The Road Not Taken' and answer the questions.

And both that morning equally lay
In leaves no step had trodden black.
Oh, I kept the first for another day!
Yet knowing how way leads on to way,
I doubted if I should ever come back.

I shall be telling this with a sigh
Somewhere ages and ages hence:
Two roads diverged in a wood, and I—
I took the one less traveled by,
And that has made all the difference.

1. Draw lines to link the quotation with the correct explanation.

Quotation	What does this tell us about the journey we take in life?
'And both that morning equally lay/In leaves no step had trodden black'	The speaker thinks that they will return and perhaps take the first path one day.
'Oh, I kept the first for another day!'	The speaker knows that they may regret this choice in later life.
'Yet knowing how way leads on to way/I doubted if I should ever come back.	The speaker knows that once choices are made it is hard to go back.
'I shall be telling this with a sigh/Somewhere ages and ages hence:'	The paths are equally covered in leaves so the speaker can't follow anyone's route or ask for advice.

2. Look at the final two lines of the poem. What are we told about the decision?

_____

_____

Language Choices in Non-fiction

Key Word
information text

↺ Recap

When you are writing to inform, you need to organise and link ideas clearly and concisely. This style of writing is often used in leaflets, some newspaper articles and textbooks.

📄 Revise

In this newspaper article, the writer is informing readers about Mike Perham's achievement in being the youngest person to sail around the world. This is the purpose of the text.

The topic sentence introduces the focus for the newspaper report.

17 year-old Mike Perham became the youngest person to sail single-handed around the world this morning. His 50 ft yacht Totallymoney.com crossed the finish line at 09:47:30 local time.

Additional factual details. A clear and concise sentence.

The information below comes from a website that helps potential owners choose the right dog breed for their lifestyle. This is the purpose of the text.

Border Terrier

This is one of the most popular terrier breeds, Border Terriers, with their otter-like heads, are small- to medium-sized terriers. To begin with, bred to help Foxhounds with hunting, these dogs are quick, enjoy digging and tend to have a strong prey drive.

The topic sentence introduces the subject of the **information text**: Border Terrier dogs. This sentence also gives three facts about these dogs: their popularity, the shape of their heads and their size.

Information about how the breed originated is followed by three facts about how the dogs behave.

When making language choices in non-fiction texts, remember:

- The need to be clear will influence the length of your sentences.
- You can use subheadings to organise content.
- Try to order paragraphs in a logical way to help ensure your text is clear.

✔ Check

Read the extract from an article about the King's coronation weekend and answer the questions.

A balcony appearance at Buckingham Palace, a UK-wide light show and a concert featuring global stars formed the celebrations for the King's coronation.

The palace delivered an exciting schedule of events which took place over the coronation weekend from Saturday, May 6 to Monday, May 8.

What happened?

[…]

Sunday, May 7

Sunday saw 'global music icons and contemporary stars' descend on Windsor Castle for the coronation concert, which was broadcast live.

Several thousand members of the public were selected to receive a pair of free tickets through a national ballot held by the BBC.

The show featured a world-class orchestra fronted by 'some of the world's biggest entertainers, alongside performers from the world of dance.'

There was also the Coronation Choir, a diverse group that was created from the nation's keenest community choirs and amateur singers from across the UK.

1. In paragraphs 1–3, four different events are mentioned that took place over the weekend. What were they?

_____

_____

2. When did the events take place?

_____

3. Find an example of a question used to organise information.

_____

4. What information were we given about the events on Sunday May 7?

_____

_____

_____

_____

_____

Figurative and Poetic Language

↺ Recap

Writers use language to express their ideas and viewpoints. Figurative and poetic language can be used in non-fiction as well as fiction texts to influence readers.

🗐 Revise

In *Forget Me Not*, Sophie Pavelle, a science writer, embarks on a low-carbon journey across Britain to find animals and habitats that are threatened by climate change. Here, she introduces the reader to seagrass, a saltwater plant.

The topic sentence introduces the type of plant – seagrass – and shows its importance to humankind: swimming with it 'could rank in the top five of the great human experiences'.

Use of 'we' to include the reader in this experience.

Nature is personified as being stifled by internet diversions.

Two short sentences change the **rhythm** and reinforce the key point about plants.

An **oxymoron** is used to convey the fierce happiness mixed with gentle affection that nature can bring to people.

An anecdote is used to illustrate the unexciting elements of nature watching. Elements that the reader can relate to.

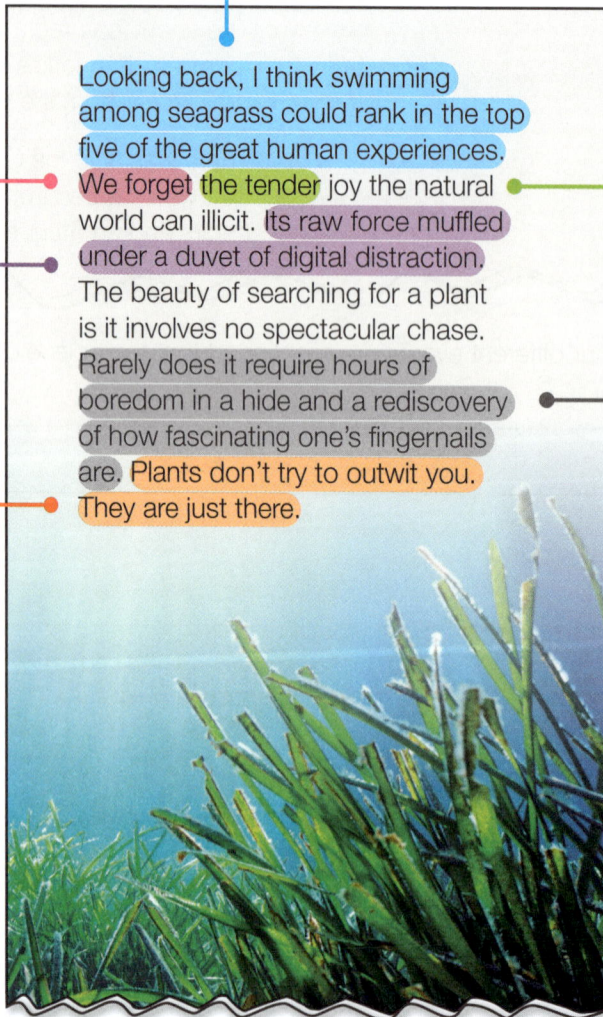

> Looking back, I think swimming among seagrass could rank in the top five of the great human experiences. We forget the tender joy the natural world can illicit. Its raw force muffled under a duvet of digital distraction. The beauty of searching for a plant is it involves no spectacular chase. Rarely does it require hours of boredom in a hide and a rediscovery of how fascinating one's fingernails are. Plants don't try to outwit you. They are just there.

When you are analysing a writer's language choices, always explain *why* the writer is using the device.

✔ Check

In this extract, Sophie Pavelle describes a merlin – a tiny falcon that can be found in the UK.

Read the text and answer the questions.

Exploding from their lookout post, a merlin hunts with immense purpose and hustle – rarely will it glide like a buzzard or hover like a kestrel. Instead, the merlin uses fast, powerful wing beats, interspersed with short, precise glides, to help it stay fiercely loyal to a low airborne course while it scans for prey. As a rule, all hawks have incredible vision. A kestrel can spot a dor beetle 50 metres away. It (and many other species, too) can detect ultraviolet light, invisible to the naked human eye, affording it a window into the urine trails of small mammals. Handy, if a vole is their snack of choice!

1. How is the merlin's flight pattern different to a kestrel's or buzzard's flight pattern?

_____

_____

_____

2. Draw lines to link each quotation with the correct language analysis.

Quotation	Language analysis
As a rule	contrast to illustrate the differences between the bird and human abilities
It (and many other species, too) can detect ultraviolet light, invisible to the naked human eye	direct language to give factual information to the reader
A kestrel can spot a dor beetle 50 metres away.	metaphor shows the powerful burst of the bird's movement
Exploding from their lookout post,	conversational language as if chatting with the reader
Handy, if a vole is their snack of choice!	lighthearted comment emphasising the purposeful nature of the bird

Structure in Poetry

↻ Recap

Poetry can have a variety of forms. **Poetic form** is part of a poem's structure and gives it shape and meaning.

Elements that contribute to structure include:

- a story or argument
- stanzas
- the **rhyme scheme**
- rhythm
- **line length**
- a series of images.

📋 Revise

The poem is written as a sonnet – a 14-line poem with a tight structure.

The narrator tells a traveller that he found the legs of a huge statue in the desert. A broken head was nearby. An inscription reveals that Ozymandias had been a powerful ruler.

The sonnet can be split into two sections. In the first eight lines (octave), the traveller describes the broken and crumbling statue.

There are three voices in the poem: the narrator, the traveller and Ozymandias.

The voice of Ozymandias enters in the final six lines (sestet). This structure enables Shelley to reveal his key message: however boastful you are about your power, it will always crumble into dust.

Ozymandias

I met a traveller from an antique land,
Who said – "Two vast and trunkless legs of stone
Stand in the desert…. Near them, on the sand,
Half sunk a shattered visage lies, whose frown,
And wrinkled lip, and sneer of cold command,
Tell that its sculptor well those passions read
Which yet survive, stamped on these lifeless things,
The hand that mocked them, and the heart that fed;
And on the pedestal, these words appear:
My name is Ozymandias, King of Kings;
Look on my Works, ye Mighty, and despair!
Nothing beside remains. Round the decay
Of that colossal Wreck, boundless and bare
The lone and level sands stretch far away."

Percy Bysshe Shelley
(1792–1822)

✔ Check

Read 'The Eagle' by Alfred, Lord Tennyson, then answer the questions.

> He clasps the crag with crooked hands;
> Close to the sun in lonely lands,
> Ring'd with the azure world, he stands.
>
> The wrinkled sea beneath him crawls;
> He watches from his mountain walls,
> And like a thunderbolt he falls.

> Look for patterns in a poem. This will help you to identify its structure.

1. What is the poem about? _____

2. The poem is divided into two stanzas. What is the eagle doing in each stanza?

   Stanza 1: _____

   Stanza 2: _____

3. These statements focus on the rhyme scheme. Circle the best statement. Explain why you chose it.

   The rhyme scheme is unusual as there is only one set of rhymes in each stanza.

   In stanza 1, all of the lines end in –ands. In stanza 2, all of the words end in –alls.

   The rhyme scheme is tight and controlled using only one rhyme in each stanza. This reflects the power of the eagle as he moves from watcher to fierce hunter.

   _____
   _____

4. a. Look at the final line of the first stanza: 'Ring'd with the azure world, he stands'. Now look again at the last line of the second stanza: 'And like a thunderbolt he falls'. What contrast is shown?

   _____

   b. What impact does this contrast have on the reader?

   _____
   _____
   _____

Structure in Non-fiction

↻ Recap

Non-fiction articles often contain these structural features:

- an engaging title to catch the reader's attention
- an opening paragraph that gives an overview of the subject
- subheadings to help organise the content
- paragraphs in an effective order
- a convincing conclusion.

📄 Revise

This article is from a veterinary website; it is written by a medical expert. Its purpose is to inform. The audience would be pet owners, probably adults.

> The title is posed as a question to catch the reader's attention.

Can dogs be vegan?

Veganism is rising in popularity among humans, but can our canine friends benefit from such a diet?

To know whether dogs can be vegans, it's important to understand their dietary needs.

Let's take a closer look.

So, can dogs be vegan?

Technically, yes, dogs can be vegan – but 'technically' is the operative word here. Whilst it is possible for a dog to survive on a meat-free diet, this doesn't necessarily mean plant-based diets for dogs should be encouraged.

> A second question is used to establish the line of argument.

> An authoritative tone, setting out the line of argument.

> Notice the pattern of posing a question and then answering the question to structure the article.

The structure helps to guide the reader through the text and establishes a clear line of argument.

✔ Check

Read the conclusion of the article and answer the questions.

A vegan dog diet – does it exist?

So yes, technically it does. Think of it like this though: vegan diets for dogs are *possible*, but VERY hard to get right. Unless you've been advised otherwise by a vet, your dog should eat a high-quality, complete and balanced diet that includes meat as part of a range of ingredients.

If you decided to put your dog on a meat-free diet without contacting your vet for advice, you'd put them at risk of multiple dietary deficiencies and health problems. If you did it with the help of a vet or nutritionist, you'd have to follow their advice very carefully.

Because of the effort, time and expense involved with this, it's recommended that dogs should only become 'vegans' as a last resort. It's not something you should strive for!

---

1. Give one example of how the writer uses questions to structure the text.

_____

2. In this final section, the writer makes a series of points. Sort the points into the correct structure by numbering them from 1–5.

Dogs should only become vegans as a last resort. ☐

Vegan diets for dogs can be expensive and difficult to follow. ☐

Contact a vet before using vegan diets; otherwise you could put your dog at risk. ☐

Dogs should eat meat unless advised by a vet. ☐

A vegan diet does exist but is hard to get right. ☐

Rhetorical Devices in Non-fiction

Key Words

rhetorical devices

↺ Recap

Writers of speeches and other non-fiction texts often use **rhetorical devices** and emotive language to influence the reader's or audience's reactions.

📝 Revise

This is an extract from the start of Greta Thunberg's speech at the UN climate action summit in 2016. The speech is a response to a question about the message she has for world leaders.

A list of three statements emphasising that it is wrong that she has to be there.

> This is all wrong. I shouldn't be up here. I should be back in school on the other side of the ocean. Yet you all come to us young people for hope. How dare you!
>
> You have stolen my dreams and my childhood with your empty words. And yet I'm one of the lucky ones. People are suffering. People are dying. Entire ecosystems are collapsing. We are in the beginning of a mass extinction, and all you can talk about is money and fairy tales of eternal economic growth. How dare you!

Emotive language to inspire a feeling or reaction.

An exclamation is used to shock.

A list of three statements is used to emphasise the negative consequences, including the repetition of 'People' for emphasis.

Mockery is used to devalue the UN leaders' focus on economic impact. The reference to 'fairy tales' highlights the contrast in their ages. She could be expected to listen to fairy tales – yet it is the adults who are listening to fairy tales.

Repeated exclamation for emphasis.

✔ Check

Read the extract from the end of Greta Thunberg's speech and answer the questions.

How dare you pretend that this can be solved with business as usual and some technical solutions!

With today's emissions levels, that remaining CO_2 budget will be entirely gone within less than 8.5 years.

There will not be any solutions or plans presented in line with these figures here today. Because these numbers are too uncomfortable. And you are still not mature enough to tell it like it is.

Your generation is failing us. But the young people are starting to understand your betrayal. The eyes of all future generations are upon you.

And if you choose to fail us, I say we will never forgive you.

We will not let you get away with this. Right here, right now is where we draw the line.

The world is waking up.

And change is coming, whether you like it or not.

1. Find one example of each of these devices.

Use of figures to support ideas/argument	
Suggestion of group involvement by using 'us'/'we'	
Issue of a warning – change now or this will happen	
Use of a three-part list for emphasis	

2. What is the tone of this speech? Explain why you think this.

_____

_____

Figurative Devices in Fiction

↻ Recap

Figurative language uses devices such as similes, metaphors, **alliteration**, onomatopoeia and **personification** to help writers explore complex ideas and create rich texts.

🗎 Revise

Let's look at how Scrooge is portrayed in *A Christmas Carol* by Charles Dickens.

Figurative device	Definition	Quotation	Meaning
Simile	Comparison using 'like' or 'as'	'candles were flaring in the windows of the neighbouring offices, like ruddy smears upon the palpable brown air.'	Even though the candles are 'flaring', the night is so gloomy they appear as 'ruddy smears'; dirty marks on the windows.
Metaphor	Direct comparison – using 'is' or 'was'	'he iced his office'	Scrooge's presence makes the atmosphere in his office icy and unpleasant.
Alliteration	Repeated consonant sounds for effect	'No warmth could warm, nor wintry weather chill him.'	The repeated 'w' sound emphasises Scrooge's cold and wintry nature.
Onomatopoeia	Sounds like what it's describing	'ding dong, bell. Bell,'	The clamour of bells suggests a sense of hope as Scrooge seeks to make amends for his actions.
Personification	An object or a feeling described in human terms	'His own heart laughed'	Scrooge is so happy that even his heart is laughing along with him.

It is important to explain why the writer has used figurative devices. What does the writer want the reader to understand?

✔ Check

Read the extracts from *A Christmas Carol* by Charles Dickens, then answer the questions.

> Hard and sharp as flint, from which no steel had ever struck out generous fire; secret, and self-contained, and solitary as an oyster.

1. Dickens uses the simile 'solitary as an oyster' to describe Scrooge.

   a. What does 'solitary' mean? _____

   b. What is an oyster like? _____

   c. What does 'solitary as an oyster' tell us about Scrooge?

   _____

   _____

2. Dickens uses another simile to describe Scrooge in this extract.

   a. What is the simile? _____

   b. What does this simile tell us about Scrooge?

   _____

> It must have run there when it was a young house, playing at hide-and-seek with other houses and have forgotten the way out again. It was old enough now, and dreary enough; for nobody lived in it but Scrooge, the other rooms all being let out as offices.

3. a. What figurative device is Dickens using? _____

   b. What does this extract tell us about Scrooge's home?

   _____

   _____

   c. Dickens says that no one lives in the house other than Scrooge. What does this suggest about Scrooge?

   _____

   _____

Personal Letters

↻ Recap

You might write a personal letter to a friend or a relative. Personal letters have a specific layout (form). You need to consider the person you are writing to (audience) and the reason why you are writing the letter (purpose).

📋 Revise

10 Grange Road
Liverpool
L6 4PT

Bhavna's address

16th April 2023

The date the letter was written

Hello Ria,

An informal greeting

After recently listening to you talk about going to live abroad, I have been thinking about how my life will change without you.

This is the body of the letter. It begins with a topic sentence that states why Bhavna is writing the letter.

I first met you in high school where we became very close friends. You have always been my closest friend and I am devastated that you are talking about moving abroad!

I have got some great memories, especially being part of drama club and going on day trips to the beach. Remember when we camped out during activities week? There was such freedom being able to watch the stars.

The main ideas and line of argument are usually outlined in two or three paragraphs.

I think going to live abroad is such a big step. Among other changes, you will have to find a whole set of new friends. As you know, I disagree very much with you moving there, but at the end of the day it is your decision and your future.

I hope whatever decision you make is the right one and will make you happy.

The final paragraph sums up the argument.

Good luck!

Bhavna

An informal phrase signs off the letter.

The purpose of the letter and the audience help you to set the tone and steer your language choices.

✔ Check

Here's a plan and notes for a personal letter to a friend who has been offered the opportunity to study abroad. The purpose of the letter is to give your opinion on whether they should take the opportunity.

Paragraph 1: Briefly outline the issue and state your opinion.

Paragraph 2: Give reasons why this is an exciting opportunity.

Paragraph 3: Acknowledge their worries and give advice.

Paragraph 4: Brief statement of your opinion and state you will see them soon.

1. Write an opening one-sentence paragraph that outlines that you have heard about this opportunity and you think they should take it.

_____

_____

2. Put a tick in each row of the table, showing whether you would use each point in paragraph 2 (P2) or 3 (P3) of the letter.

Notes	P2	P3
I know you will miss your friends but we can video call as often as you want.		
What a great opportunity this is!		
It might seem that it's a long way away, but flights are available and are easy to work out.		
There will be so many new foods to try and new sights to see.		
Imagine being fluent in another language!		
It is only two years. Time will fly.		

3. Write paragraph 4 of the letter, using the plan to help you. Remember it should be brief.

_____

_____

Formal Letters

↻ Recap

You might write a formal letter to a business or person in authority. Formal letters have a specific layout (form). You need to consider the person you are writing to (audience) and the reason why you are writing the letter (purpose).

📄 Revise

10 Oxlea Road
Exeter
EX6 9LP

The Editor
Devon News Magazine
Exeter

16th April 2023

Dear Sir or Madam,

I would like to complain about an article, 'All out of control', that appeared in your magazine on 14th April.

In this article your reporter claimed that a group of students from St Martin's High School were 'marauding' in a local park after school. You said that young people were fighting and shouting. I would like to point out that this was, in fact, the school drama club who were rehearsing a scene from their new production of *West Side Story*. We had obtained permission from the local residents' group and at no point did your reporter try to find out what was actually happening.

This type of publicity is very damaging for our school. As a student body we are proud to be part of an innovative school community and work hard to support charities. The proceeds from our school production will be supporting ActionAid.

I hope to see a full retraction in the magazine and would like to invite your theatre critic to our upcoming production.

Yours faithfully,

Armin Biswas

Armin's address

The address of the business Armin is writing to

The date the letter was written

A formal greeting

The letter begins with a topic sentence that states why Armin is writing the letter.

The main ideas and line of argument are usually outlined in two or three paragraphs.

The final paragraph clearly states the future action that Armin expects.

A formal sign-off

If you start a formal letter with Dear Sir or Madam, end with Yours faithfully.

If you start a formal letter with Dear [Name], end with Yours sincerely.

✔ Check

Here's a plan and notes for a formal letter to apply for a Saturday job at the local newsagent. The purpose of the letter is to outline why you would be suitable for the job.

Paragraph 1: Briefly outline where you saw the job advertised and that you would like to apply for the job.

Paragraph 2: Outline the personal qualities that make you suitable for the job.

Paragraph 3: Outline the work and school experience that make you suitable for the job.

Paragraph 4: Sum up by thanking them and mention the interview.

1. Write an opening one-sentence paragraph that outlines where you saw the job advertised and that you would like to apply for it.

_____

_____

2. Put a tick in each row of the table, showing whether you would use each point in paragraph 2 (P2) or 3 (P3) of the letter.

Notes	P2	P3
I am a reliable worker and know that you could rely on me in this role.		
My participation in school sports teams means that I am a team player and know how to work alongside others.		
I am calm under pressure and can make decisions quickly when I need to.		
I have had a paper round for the past year and have learned how to manage my time effectively.		
I like working as part of a team and enjoy meeting new people.		
I am a member of the school council and am used to talking with adults in a range of situations.		

3. Write paragraph 4 of the letter, using the plan to help you. Remember it should be brief.

_____

_____

Writing Articles

↺ Recap

When you write articles for newspapers and magazines, you need to think about the purpose of the article (why it's being written), the audience (who it's written for) and the form (how it looks and its features).

🗒 Revise

Look at the start of an article from a children's news website. Think about purpose, audience and form.

Form: engaging headline to catch attention and introduce the topic.

Form: opening paragraph gives an overview of the topic.

Purpose and audience: use of interesting facts to engage and inform.

Trees can talk!

World-renowned German forestry expert Peter Wohlleben has boldly claimed that trees have characters and can communicate with each other.

Peter says that trees have the ability to communicate via their roots and these form an underground 'woodwide web'.

Their communication goes beyond just talking, he believes that trees can send signals to warn each other if they are attacked by disease and to cut down on water if supplies are low.

Purpose: to inform and entertain.

Audience: young people.

Form: paragraphs are in an effective order to organise ideas.

As with writing formal and informal letters, the purpose and audience help you to set the tone for writing articles and steer your language choices.

✔ Check

Here are notes for an article informing primary pupils about their first day at secondary school. The purpose is to inform and reassure the pupils.

Paragraph 1: It is normal to be worried but there will be help and support.

Paragraph 2: The support that will be on offer on your first day.

Paragraph 3: What you can do to get ready and help yourself during the day.

1. Put a tick in each row of the table, showing whether you would use each point in paragraph 1 (P1), 2 (P2) or 3 (P3) of the article.

Notes	P1	P3	P3
Everyone is nervous on the first day.			
Make sure you have equipment for the day, such as a pen, reading book.			
You will be given a map to help you navigate the school.			
Everyone has had a first day at school – even the teachers.			
Make your packed lunch or snack the night before.			
Is your uniform labelled with your name? Schools have lots of students and things often get lost.			
Your tutor will give you a copy of your timetable – don't lose it!			
You will be tired after your first day – get an early night!			
Practise your journey to school.			
There will be systems in place to help and support you.			
Teachers will explain what happens in class and what you can expect from each subject.			
Everyone gets lost!			

2. Using the notes above, write your own article in a separate notebook. Write a suitable headline for the article.

Speeches

↺ Recap

Speeches have a specific form and use specific conventions. You need to think about who you are talking to (audience) and the reason why you are speaking (purpose). Often, speeches are persuasive.

📑 Revise

This is a speech from the head of the student council informing KS3 students about the school's new revision programme and persuading them to take part.

Good afternoon Key Stage 3. We are here today to spark your interest in our new revision programme.

Clear address to audience.

Why do we need to begin our revision now? This is the crucial stage. It is the tipping point of whether we win or lose; pass or fail; get to where we want to be or fall by the wayside.

Rhetorical devices are used throughout the speech.

Revision is an active event. Like people who go to a gym, we need to show up in order to develop. Map out 30 minutes a day for active revision and you will see results.

What is active revision? It's a planned series of focused tasks that help you to engage with your learning. Reading alone won't help you. Only engaging with the content through quizzes, flash cards and knowing how the exam works will help you succeed.

Sections/paragraphs are in a convincing order.

We will seize this opportunity.

A convincing conclusion.

Thank you for listening to these important ideas and I hope they will spur you to action.

This is a clear sign-off, directly addressing the audience.

See pages 44–45 for further information on rhetorical devices.

Make sure that you know the audience for and purpose of your speech before you begin writing.

✔ Check

Here are notes for a speech to the governing body of your school, with the purpose of persuading them to increase the time for PE on the timetable.

Paragraph 1: Address governors

Paragraph 2: Outline current situation, including numbers of students who do sports clubs outside school

Paragraph 3: Health risks and outcomes

Paragraph 4: Benefits of physical activity on health and well-being

Paragraph 5: Sign-off directly addressing governors

1. Write the opening address to governors from paragraph 1.

_____

_____

2. Which of these statements including statistics is most useful for paragraph 2? Circle your response.

Football is the most popular team sport to participate in, with roughly 1.5 million people in England playing at least twice per month.

Across 5–15-year-olds, 81.6% do sport. 77.8% take part in school and 37.9% take part outside school.

The number of women who currently play sport or who closely follow sporting events is steadily increasing. This increase is a result of changes that took place in schools in the 1970s.

3. Outline three benefits of increased physical activity for young people that you could use in paragraph 4.

_____

_____

_____

4. In a separate notebook, use the five-paragraph structure above to write your own speech on a subject that you feel passionate about. For example, school lunch menus, banning single-use plastics, animal welfare issues.

Planning a Narrative

↺ Recap

When you plan a narrative, you need to think about the **genre** of the narrative (the style of the story), the audience and the **narrative structure** (the order of events and how they take place).

📄 Revise

Here is an example of narrative structure.

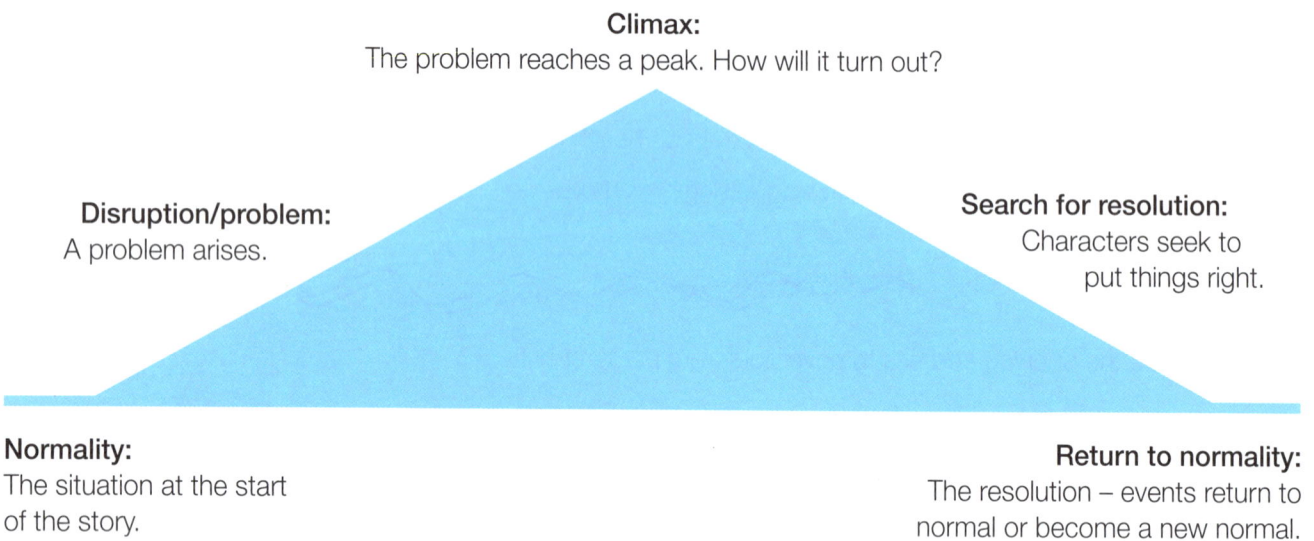

Climax:
The problem reaches a peak. How will it turn out?

Disruption/problem:
A problem arises.

Search for resolution:
Characters seek to put things right.

Normality:
The situation at the start of the story.

Return to normality:
The resolution – events return to normal or become a new normal.

This structure can be used to plan your narrative.

Look at this plan. Do you recognise the story?

Narrative structure	Story section
Normality	Two families have been fighting for generations.
Disruption/problem	A boy from one family and a girl from another family fall in love and marry in secret.
Climax	The boy commits a murder and is sent away. A marriage is arranged for the girl with a wealthy man.
Search for resolution	The girl fakes her own death. The boy believes the girl is dead and poisons himself. The girl is so upset she kills herself.
Return to normality	The families resolve their feud while mourning their children.

When you feel confident using the narrative structure, you can begin to move elements of the structure around. For example, you could begin with the return to normality and tell your story as a flashback.

✔ Check

1. Draw lines to link each story section with the correct part of the narrative structure.

Narrative structure	Story section
Normality	The warrior is given a prophecy that he will become king one day. With his wife he decides to kill the king so that the prophecy will become true.
Disruption/problem	The warrior king begins to feel insecure in his position and commits terrible murders to keep his power. The nobles turn against him.
Climax	The warrior kills the king and takes over as the new king.
Search for resolution	The nobles kill the warrior king and put another king in his place.
Return to normality	A warrior wins a battle and is given titles and lands by the king.

2. Plan a story beginning with the words: 'I realised it was a mistake as soon as I turned the corner.'

Normality	
Disruption/problem	
Climax	
Search for resolution	
Return to normality	

3. In a separate notebook, write your narrative using the plan.

Planning a Description

↻ Recap

Descriptive writing asks you to paint a picture with words. It is important to remember that this is not a story. You need to generate ideas and then plan each paragraph.

📄 Revise

Ask yourself questions to help generate ideas for a four-part plan.

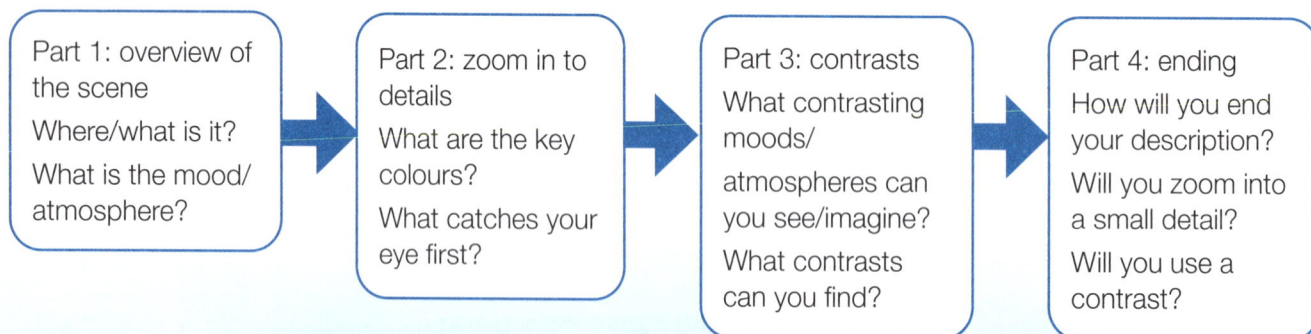

Part 1: overview of the scene	Part 2: zoom in to details	Part 3: contrasts	Part 4: ending
Where/what is it?	What are the key colours?	What contrasting moods/ atmospheres can you see/imagine?	How will you end your description?
What is the mood/ atmosphere?	What catches your eye first?	What contrasts can you find?	Will you zoom into a small detail?
			Will you use a contrast?

Your answers to these questions will help you to plan a four-part response.

Here is an example plan for a beach scene.

Plan	Description
Part 1: overview of the scene	sunny beach in the morning deserted light and breezy; full of promise for the day to come
Part 2: zoom in to details	the sea and the sky match colours an upturned boat is longing to go out to sea the cliffs - stark and proud
Part 3: contrasts	people begin to arrive windbreaks and towels contrast with the blue of the sea and sky a lost child begins to cry in fear a dog begins to bark
Part 4: ending	zoom in - child now back with parents happily eating ice-cream small detail - in the distance, a cloud appears

Remember that most of our impressions come through the things we see and hear. Drawing on the senses will make your descriptions vivid.

✔ Check

You are going to write a description of a busy market scene. You can use the image to help you – or your imagination.

1. Fill in the plan, using the questions to help you. Add as much detail as you can.

Plan	Description
Part 1: overview of the scene Where/what is it? What is the mood/atmosphere?	
Part 2: zoom in to details What are the key colours? What catches your eye first?	
Part 3: contrasts What contrasting moods/atmospheres can you see/imagine? What contrasts can you find?	
Part 4: ending How will you end your description? Will you zoom into a small detail? Will you use a contrast?	

2. In a separate notebook, write the description using your plan.

Formal and Informal Register

↻ Recap

In your writing, you can vary the levels of formality to suit the audience, purpose and context.

🗒 Revise

Formal register can include anything from legal documents to letters of complaint. Formal situations usually mean you use Standard English. This is language that you might read in broadsheet newspapers and textbooks, and that you might hear in news reports and documentaries. Formal register uses vocabulary that is relevant to the topic (for example, technical language). It is often used in business settings.

Look at this example.

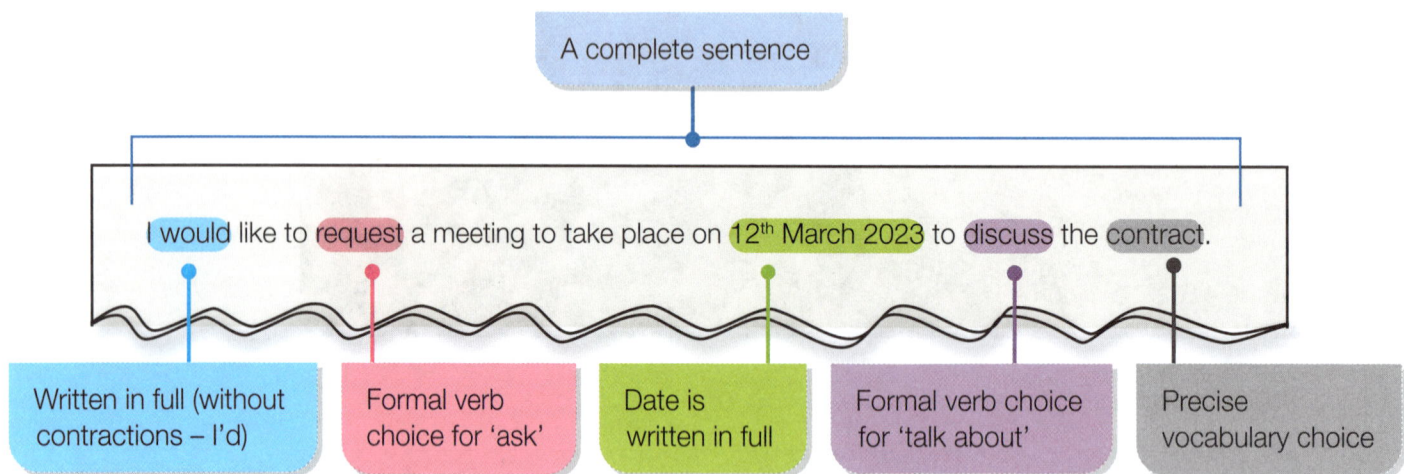

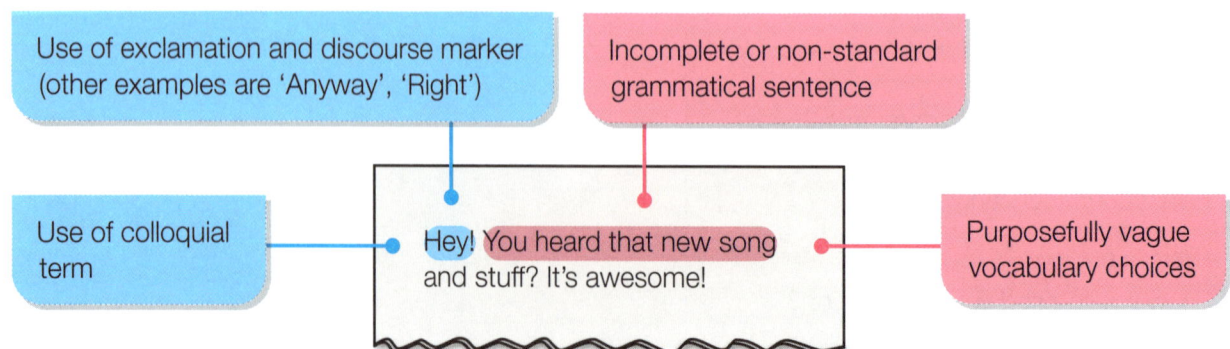

A complete sentence

I would like to request a meeting to take place on 12th March 2023 to discuss the contract.

Written in full (without contractions – I'd)

Formal verb choice for 'ask'

Date is written in full

Formal verb choice for 'talk about'

Precise vocabulary choice

Informal register can include anything from social media posts to letters to relatives and friends. Its tone is conversational and may include **contractions** (for example, wouldn't, he'll). Informal language may also include colloquial language, such as 'dimpsey' to describe fading light, 'Where's it to?' meaning 'Where is it?' and abbreviations (such as e.g., etc).

Look at this example.

Use of exclamation and discourse marker (other examples are 'Anyway', 'Right')

Incomplete or non-standard grammatical sentence

Use of colloquial term

Hey! You heard that new song and stuff? It's awesome!

Purposefully vague vocabulary choices

You will use a mixture of formal and informal register daily. Standard English is an important part of formal writing. Think of the purpose and audience for your writing or speech.

✔ Check

1. Draw lines to show which statements are formal and informal.

I am writing to complain…

Informal   What d'ya mean?

I'm not going.

The palace was dark.

Formal   I've never had a proper job.

It has been announced that…

2. Write these statements using formal register.

I've not eaten nothing. _____

Wow you're here! _____

Gimme that hoodie. _____

Wanna come play footie? _____

Ow! That hurt! _____

3. You witnessed an incident at lunchtime where a student was hurt. Write the first paragraph of your statement for the school head teacher. Choose your register.

_____

_____

_____

_____

_____

_____

Sentence Structures

Key Words
simple sentence
subject
compound sentence
complex sentence
main clause

↺ Recap

It is important to recognise and use a range of sentences to understand how a writer makes their writing interesting.

🗐 Revise

A sentence can be simple, compound or complex.

A **simple sentence** is made up of one clause containing a **subject** and a verb.

For example:

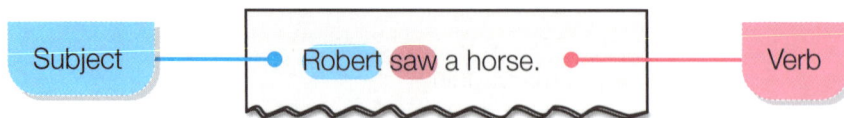

| Subject | → | Robert saw a horse. | ← | Verb |

A **compound sentence** is made up of two or more clauses linked by a **coordinating conjunction**, such as 'and', 'but', 'or'. Each clause has equal weight.

For example:

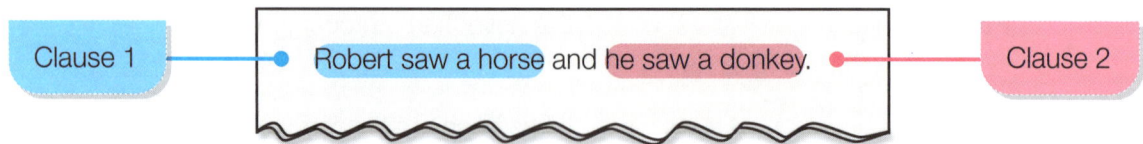

| Clause 1 | → | Robert saw a horse and he saw a donkey. | ← | Clause 2 |

A **complex sentence** is made up of a **main clause** and at least one subordinate clause.

For example:

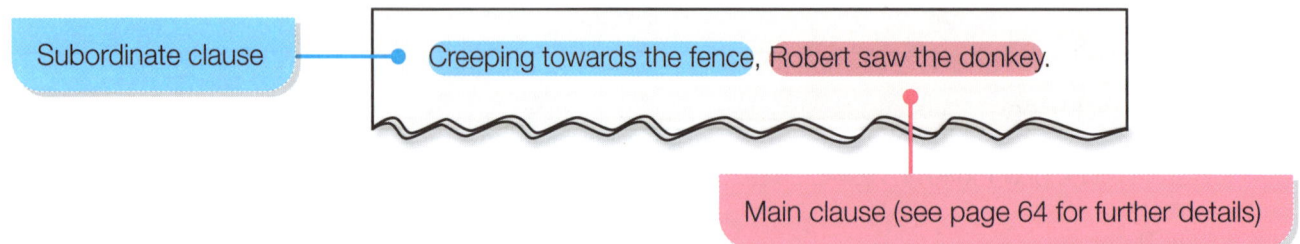

Subordinate clause → Creeping towards the fence, Robert saw the donkey.

Main clause (see page 64 for further details)

✔ Check

Identify each sentence as either a simple sentence, a compound sentence or a complex sentence.

1. The wolf howled. _____

2. As Hannah had finished her lunch, she could return to the classroom. _____

3. Apples are green but lemons are yellow. _____

4. The cat curled up tight and dreamed of hunting. _____

5. The runner was tired because they had just run a marathon. _____

Sentence Types

↻ Recap

There are four different sentence types, which all have different functions.

📋 Revise

Here are the four different sentence types:

Statement (declarative)	The girl laughed.
Question (interrogative)	Why is she laughing?
Command (imperative)	Stop laughing now.
Exclamation (exclamative)	What a laugh!

> Knowing the different sentence types will help you punctuate your sentences correctly. All statements and commands start with a capital letter and end with a full stop. Questions end with a question mark (?) and exclamations end with an exclamation mark (!).

✔ Check

1. Draw lines to link each example sentence with the correct sentence type.

Example	Sentence type	Example
Today is Monday.	statement	What a shame!
Is it Monday today?	question	The house was blue.
That hurt!		It is raining.
Go home now.	exclamation	Stop what you are doing.
Stop talking.	command	What day is it?

Punctuate the following sentences correctly.

2. where are we going

_____

3. go to the back of the classroom.

_____

4. exeter is a university city

_____

5. that's a shame

_____

Complex Sentences

Key Word
subordinate conjunction

↻ Recap

A complex sentence is made up of a main clause and one or more subordinate clauses.

📄 Revise

A main clause makes sense on its own.

For example: The girl was shouting.

A subordinate clause does not make complete sense on its own.

For example: When he arrived…

To make sense, a subordinate clause must be in a sentence with a main clause.

For example:

Subordinate clause → When he arrived, the girl was shouting. ← Main clause

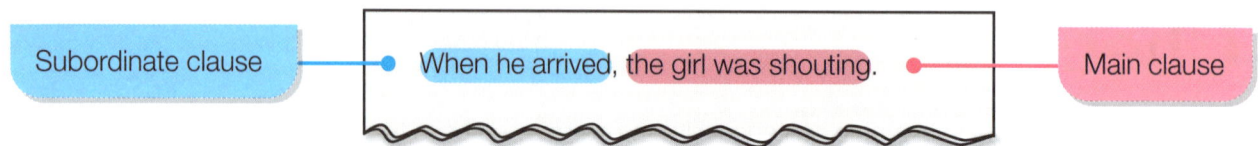

Subordinate clauses are introduced by:

- a **subordinate conjunction** such as 'if', 'because', 'as', 'when', 'unless'
- a 'wh' pronoun (for instance: He is the one *who* did it.)
- that (for example: I know *that* she did it.)
- an -ing or -ed verb (for example: *Asked* to make tea, she refused.
He marched across the playground *screaming* and *shouting*.)

Complex sentences help to link ideas and events in different ways by using subordinate conjunctions to:

- add information about time, for example, 'after', 'before', 'until', 'whenever' (for example: *After* we had eaten lunch, we went into town.)
- signal a contrast, for example, 'although', 'whereas', 'while' (for example: *Although* it was cold, we didn't wear our gloves.)
- add reasons for events or phenomena, for example, 'because', 'as', 'since', 'so' (for example: *As* the glaciers were shrinking, the terrain became more unstable.)

Subordinate clauses can be at the start of a sentence, the end of a sentence or embedded within a sentence. Here are some examples:

- Before the main clause: *After it stole the sausage*, the dog ran along the road.
- After the main clause: The dog ran along the road *after it stole the sausage*.
- Embedded: The dog, *after it stole the sausage*, ran along the road.

If you put the subordinate clause at the start of a sentence, you need to use a comma before the main clause.

If you embed the subordinate clause, you need to mark it off with commas.

✔ Check

1. Draw lines to match each subordinate clause with a main clause that you feel has most impact. Note: there is more than one possible set of answers.

Subordinate clause	Main clause
Running through the mist	the fiend managed to escape
Growling with menace	the rescuers managed to reach him
Shrouded in a thin white veil	he slunk along the corridor
Etched into the edge of the window frame	the woman vanished
Encouraged by her words	the boy called into the night
Falling through the air	the girl's life appeared before her
Tortured by memories of last night	they could identify nothing
Peering into the darkness	the dogs raced into the courtyard
Fighting a way through the crowd	the carvings were grotesque

2. Choose one of the complex sentences you have made in Question 1 and embed the subordinate clause into the main clause. Remember to use the correct punctuation.

_____

_____

3.

although	because	before	if
since	whenever	while	unless

Use a subordinate conjunction from the box to add a subordinate clause to these main clauses.

For example: If we want to make the start of the film, we have to leave immediately.

The sun was hot overhead _____

_____, we didn't wear our coats.

The dogs ran towards us _____

Relative Clauses

↺ Recap

A relative clause adds information to a noun by adapting, describing or modifying it.

📋 Revise

The relative clause begins with a **relative pronoun**: 'that', 'which', 'who', 'whom', 'whose'.

For example:

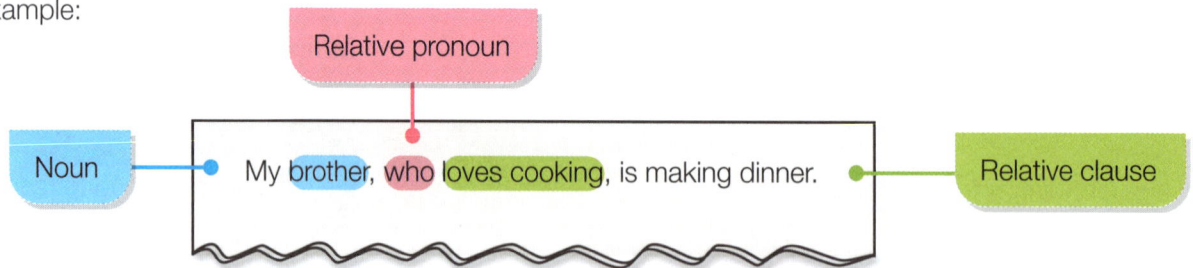

For example:

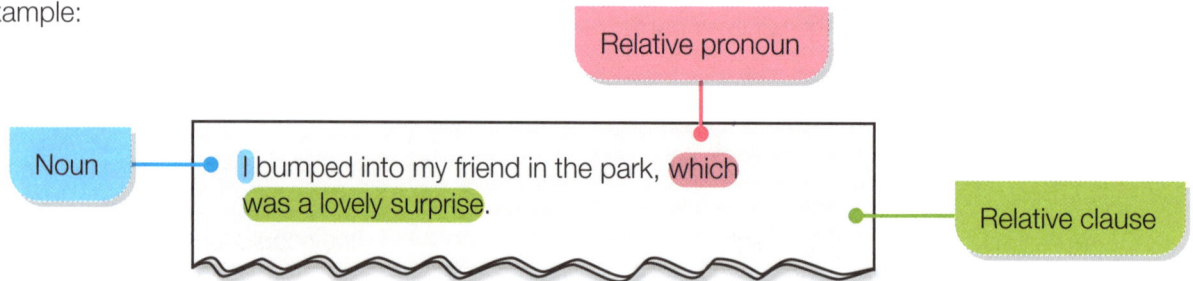

For example:

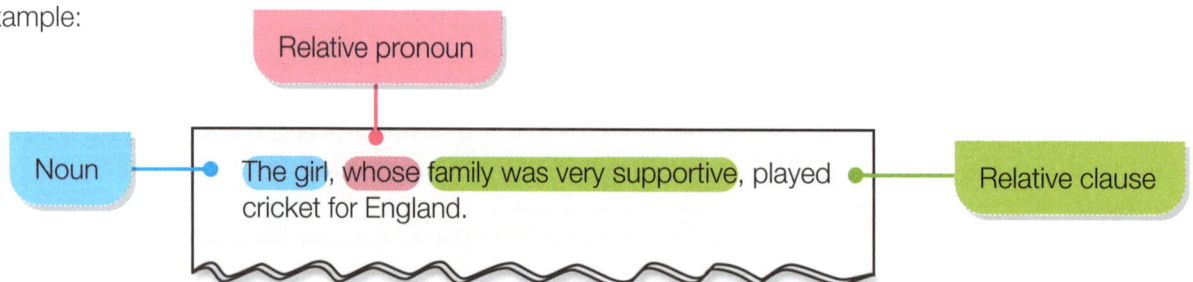

You can use 'when' and 'where' as relative pronouns when you need to clarify which time or place you are talking about.

For example:

For example:

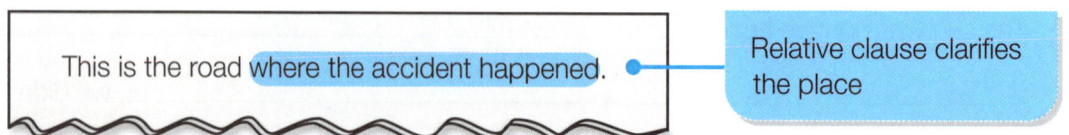

When you need to choose between 'that' or 'which', remember 'that' always refers to things and never to people.

✔ Check

Add the correct relative pronouns to these sentences.

1. The teacher, _____ was a climber, taught us rock climbing.
2. I broke the computer _____ belonged to my brother.
3. The house _____ we rented last year is empty.
4. This is the teacher _____ name I had forgotten.
5. The dog _____ hurt its leg is at the vet.

Add suitable relative clauses to these main clauses.

6. This is the school _____.
7. The library, _____, was bright and welcoming.
8. _____, I like to eat breakfast straight away.
9. Write a sentence using 'which' to make the noun more specific.

_____

_____

10. Write a sentence using 'that' to make the noun more specific.

_____

_____

whom
which that
who
whose

Using Modal Verbs

↻ Recap

Modals are **auxiliary verbs** that express ability, permission, possibility or obligation:

may	will	might	must	should	ought to
can	could	shall	would	have to	need to

📄 Revise

Modal verbs are formed by using one of these auxiliaries plus a verb. They express the degree of certainty.

For example:

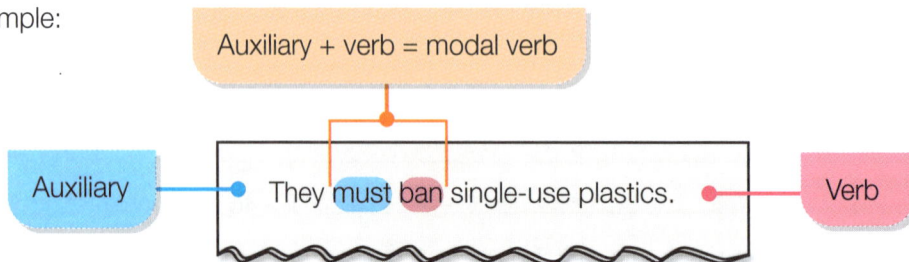

Auxiliary + verb = modal verb

Auxiliary — They must ban single-use plastics. — Verb

For example:

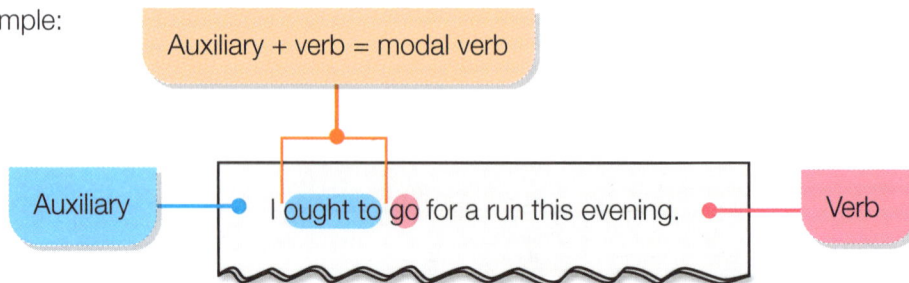

Auxiliary + verb = modal verb

Auxiliary — I ought to go for a run this evening. — Verb

✔ Check

1.

may	will	might	must	should	ought to
can	could	shall	would	have to	need to

Use a highlighter to sort these modals into two groups: those which suggest a high level of certainty and those which suggest a low degree of certainty.

2. Which of these actions is most likely to happen? Tick one box.

I could do my homework this evening. ☐   I must do my homework this evening. ☐

I will do my homework this evening. ☐   I ought to do my homework this evening. ☐

Using the Active and Passive Voice

Key Words
active voice
passive voice
object

↺ Recap

Using the **active voice** and the **passive voice** can create different points of view in your writing.

📝 Revise

In a sentence using the active voice, the subject of the sentence performs the action expressed in the verb on the **object**.

For example:

Verb

Subject → The girl frightened the boy. — Object

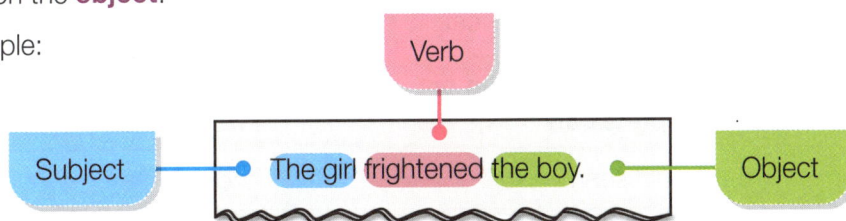

In a sentence using the passive voice, the object becomes the subject.

For example:

Verb

Subject → The boy was frightened by the girl. — Agent

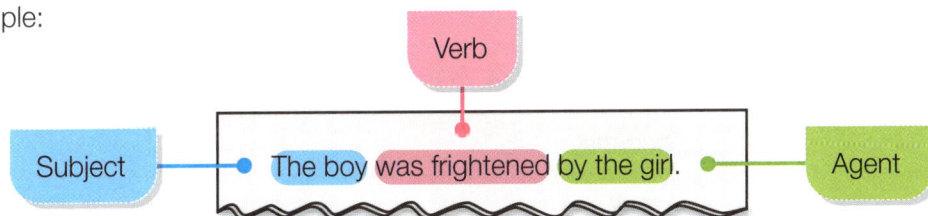

The person or thing performing an action is called the agent. Sometimes the agent can be left out completely.

For example:

Subject → The boy was frightened. — Verb

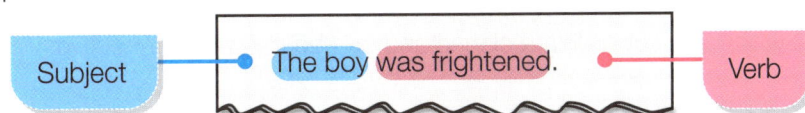

This use of the passive voice is helpful if you want to hide who was responsible for the action.

✔ Check

Change these passive sentences to active sentences. You will need to add a name or a pronoun to some of the sentences.

1. The meal was cooked by a top chef.

_____

2. The window was broken.

_____

3. A man was bitten by the dog.

_____

4. The cakes were eaten.

_____

Connecting Ideas

Key Words
connectives
conjunctions
connecting adverbials

↻ Recap

Connectives are words or phrases that help to link a text together.
They can be **conjunctions** (such as 'and', 'but', 'if'), which link clauses within sentences, or **connecting adverbials** (for example, 'also', 'however', 'furthermore'), which make links across sentences to help cohesion across the whole text.

📝 Revise

Connectives help to guide the reader and can have a specific purpose. Here are some examples.

To signal time or sequence	To signal an opinion or interpretation	To signal additional or new information
initially	it would seem	and
first/firstly	obviously	also
finally	possibly	in addition
previously	it appears	as well as
To compare	**To signal cause and effect**	**To signal a conclusion**
equally	consequently	to conclude
similarly	as a result	after all
in the same way	depending upon	in the end
likewise	inevitably	ultimately

Subordinating conjunctions introduce a subordinate clause and can be used as connectives:

after	although	as	as if
as long as	as though	because	before
if	in case	once	since
than	that	though	till
until	unless	when	whenever
where	wherever	whereas	while

Connecting adverbials link words, phrases and sentences together. They help to join your ideas.

For example:

however	moreover	nevertheless	instead	consequently

Connectives show the relationship between ideas; for example, cause and effect or the order in which events happened.

✔ Check

1. Draw lines to show which connectives are used to signal time, contrast, and cause and effect.

as a result		lastly
alternatively	**Time**	but
until		afterwards
because	**Contrast**	although
on the one hand		whenever
when	**Cause and effect**	so that

2. Select a connective from the word box to link each pair of sentences. There is more than one possible answer. Rewrite the new sentences below.

Note: you might need to put the connective before the first sentence.

For example	For instance	In spite of the fact that
Also	Furthermore	Even though
However	Although	Some may argue that
consequently	because	Instead of

There are great concerns about the environment.
No one seems to be willing to change what they do in their everyday lives.

_____

_____

_____

Almost everything that supermarkets sell is covered in plastic.
Supermarkets do not take responsibility for collecting or recycling the plastic they have sold.

_____

_____

_____

_____

We are strangling our planet with plastic.
Plastic bags litter the countryside.

_____

_____

_____

Direct Speech

↻ Recap

Direct speech means repeating the actual words of a speaker, using **speech marks**.

📄 Revise

Look at this extract from a short story called *The Monkey's Paw* by WW Jacobs.

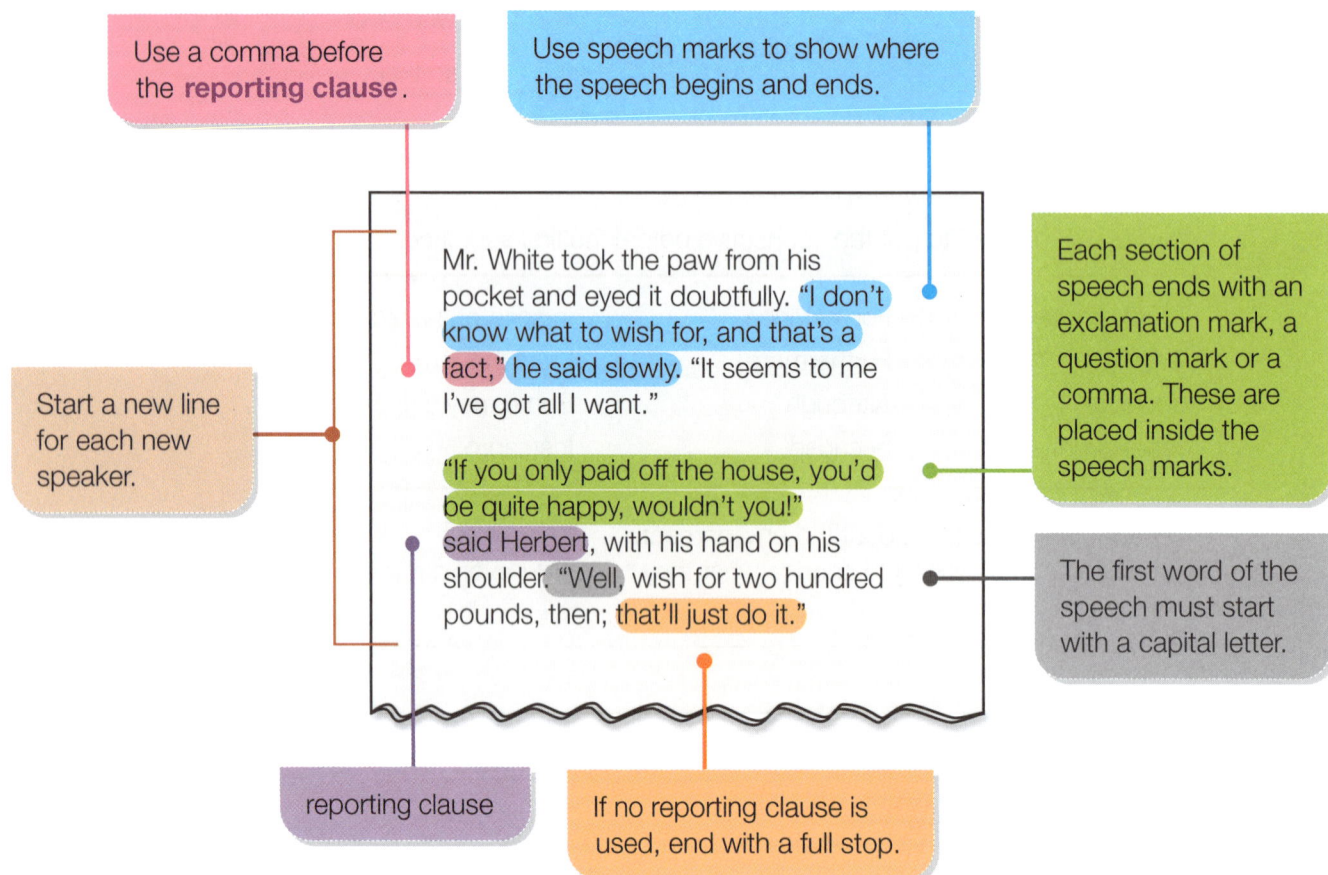

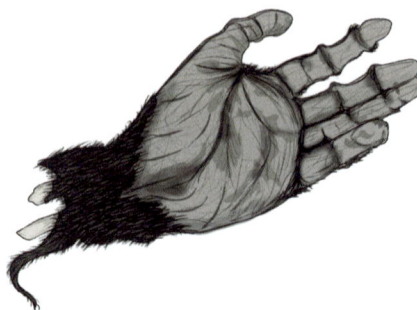

Use a comma before the **reporting clause** .

Use speech marks to show where the speech begins and ends.

Each section of speech ends with an exclamation mark, a question mark or a comma. These are placed inside the speech marks.

Start a new line for each new speaker.

Mr. White took the paw from his pocket and eyed it doubtfully. "I don't know what to wish for, and that's a fact," he said slowly. "It seems to me I've got all I want."

"If you only paid off the house, you'd be quite happy, wouldn't you!" said Herbert, with his hand on his shoulder. "Well, wish for two hundred pounds, then; that'll just do it."

The first word of the speech must start with a capital letter.

reporting clause

If no reporting clause is used, end with a full stop.

When you are writing a story, it can be useful to support speech with an action for the reader.

For example: "What?" he questioned, raising his head.

✔ Check

1. Put the punctuation in the right place.

I   am   cold   said   Kassim.

Tamsin   replied   would   you   like   to   borrow   my   jumper?

2. Put this 'knock knock' joke in the correct order. Add correct punctuation and reporting clauses.

knock knock   lettuce who   lettuce   who's there

let us in its cold out here

_____

_____

_____

_____

_____

3. Add the correct punctuation and layout to this extract from *The Monkey's Paw*.

and did you really have the three wishes granted asked Mrs. White. I did said the Sergeant-Major, and his glass tapped against his strong teeth. and has anybody else wished continued the old lady.

_____

_____

_____

_____

_____

4. Punctuate this conversation using direct speech.

Robin said that he was going to go to the park after school and invited his best friend, Pablo, to go with him. Pablo apologised and said that he was going to his swimming lesson.

_____

_____

_____

_____

Colons

Key Words
colon
independent clauses

↻ Recap

A **colon** (:) shows that the writer is about to explain or expand on what has just been written.

A colon may introduce a list of items, a long quotation, or an elaborated version of a point made in the first part of the sentence.

📋 Revise

Use a colon in your writing for:

- introducing a list

  For example:

  The following people are in the boy band BTS: RM, Jin, Suga, J-Hope, V, Jimin and Jungkook.

- joining two **independent clauses** when the second clause is directly related to the first and explains or expands what has been written

  For example:

  I explained again my reasons for not entering my bedroom: I had set a booby trap above the door.

- introducing a quotation

  For example:

  In the immortal words of BTS: "Don't be trapped in someone else's dream."

✔ Check

Rewrite these sentences, adding a colon in the correct place in each sentence.

1. I needed only three cards to win the seven of diamonds, the ace of hearts and the queen of spades.

_____

_____

2. My parents had set a new rule do your homework before using the computer.

_____

_____

3. The new school timetable had serious drawbacks students had no time to eat lunch and staff had too much marking to do.

_____

_____

4. Elephant (noun) a large grey mammal

_____

Semicolons

↻ Recap

A **semicolon** holds two grammatically complete clauses together when there is a close relationship between them. It shows that the writer is about to extend what has just been written into a slightly different but connected aspect.

A semicolon can also be used to punctuate a series of phrases already containing commas, to avoid the confusing effect of too many commas in one sentence.

You can usually replace a semicolon with another punctuation mark or a **conjunction**.

🗒 Revise

Here are examples of how a semicolon can join two grammatically complete clauses together to extend what has been written:

- Yesterday I saw a red-eyed dog; it was standing in the garden when I got home.

- My parents came home today; they had been away for a week.

Here is an example of how a semicolon can separate linked items in a list:

- Today I ate: toast and jam; a tomato and lettuce sandwich; three of Grandma's cakes and chickpea curry.

And here is one example of how you can replace a semicolon with a conjunction:

- It was raining; we didn't dawdle to school.

- It was raining so we didn't dawdle to school.

✔ Check

Rewrite these sentences, adding a semicolon in the correct place(s) in each sentence.

1. She went to the library and collected: a copy of *Dune*, the next in her favourite series an audiobook of *An Inspector Calls* and a handy revision guide.

_____

_____

_____

2. The new James Bond film is showing on Wednesday 9 May at 17:30, on Thursday 10 May at 18:30, on Friday 11 May at 12:00 and 18:30, and on Saturday 12 May at 12:00.

_____

_____

_____

_____

Parenthesis

↻ Recap

Use **parenthesis** when you want to add an idea into a sentence that is not part of the main sentence.

There are three different types of parenthesis, depending on what type of information you wish to add and what impact you want to have on the reader: brackets, dashes and commas.

📋 Revise

Brackets add non-essential information into a sentence, which can help to make the sentence clear. Brackets can have their own punctuation.

For example:

Non-essential information	My friend (who goes to another school) is coming to visit today.	Brackets enclose the information to separate it from the main idea.

For example:

My friend (the one you met last week!) is coming to visit today.	Additional punctuation to signal an exclamation sits within the brackets.

Use dashes when you want to interrupt your main idea. Dashes give more emphasis.

For example:

Dashes enclose the information to separate it from the main idea.	My friend – who is arriving any moment – goes to another school.	This text interrupts the main sentence to emphasise this point.

Commas enclose ideas that belong firmly in the flow of your sentence. Usually, this writing is more formal.

For example:

Additional information; formal tone.	My friend, who lives in London, is coming to visit today.	Commas enclose the information to separate it from the main idea.

When you remove the additional information contained within brackets, dashes and commas, your sentence should still make sense.

✔ Check

Underline the words in the sentences that should be in brackets.

For example: The boy <u>the one with blue hair</u> played guitar.

1. The dog the noisy one needs to go for a walk.

2. I went very reluctantly for a walk.

3. The football pitch owned by the club was icy.

Add additional information to these sentences, using dashes and an appropriate clause.

For example: The school – with the famous head teacher – was on the news again.

4. Jungkook _____ will be singing at the opening ceremony.

5. The hotel _____ stood on a hill.

6. The waves _____ crashed to the shore.

Add additional information and commas to these sentences.

For example: My cousin, who loved school, did well in his exams.

7. _____ whose parents were attending,

_____.

8. _____ who was 14,

_____.

9. _____ which was green,

_____.

10. _____ whom he had admired since he was young,

_____.

Apostrophes of Contraction

↺ Recap

Apostrophes of contraction signal that letters have been left out when two or more words are joined.

📄 Revise

The apostrophe shows you where the letters have been omitted.

For example:

'should not' becomes 'shouldn't'	Missing letter 'o'
'you are' becomes 'you're'	Missing letter 'a'
'he will' becomes 'he'll'	Missing letters 'w i'
'I would' becomes 'I'd'	Missing letters 'w o u l'

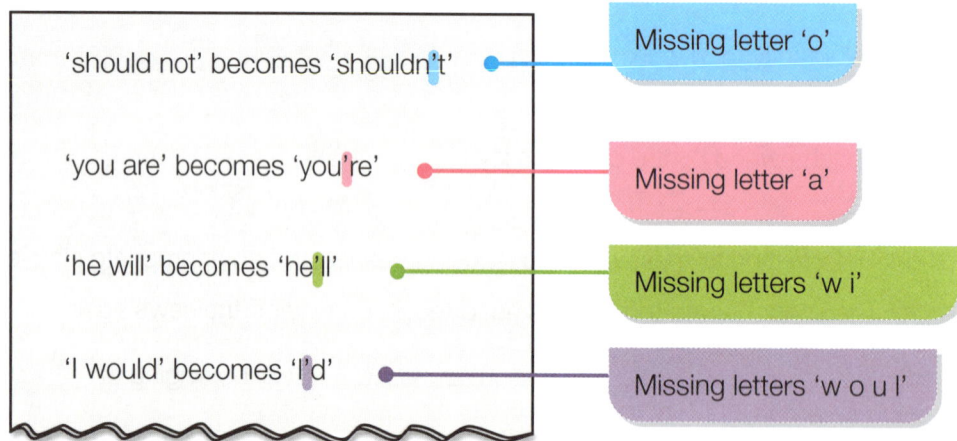

The exception to this pattern is 'will not'. This becomes 'won't'.

✔ Check

1. Write the contractions of these phrases.

was not _____   they are _____   of the clock _____

there is _____   she would _____

2. Rewrite these sentences, using apostrophes of contraction.

Tell me it its too much. _____

Whens it time for its injection? _____

Its close to the end of the film. _____

Johns unsure if its correct. _____

She should not have done that. _____

He had not had his dinner yet. _____

The dog would not have barked. _____

Apostrophes of Possession

↺ Recap

An apostrophe with the letter 's' can show **possession** – if an object belongs to someone or something. It is important to know if the subject is singular or plural, as this changes the position of the apostrophe.

📑 Revise

One girl – add 's	the girl's bag = the bag belonging to the girl
Many girls – add s'	the girls' bag = the bag belonging to the girls (plural)
If a name or object ends in the letter 's', use an apostrophe + 's' unless the last **syllable** of the name is pronounced 'iz'.	Thomas's bag Moses' lunch

You use apostrophes to show possession for nouns, for example, Ben's bag, but 'its' is a **possessive pronoun** (like 'his', 'hers', 'mine', 'theirs') and therefore you don't need an apostrophe.

✔ Check

1. Rewrite these sentences, using apostrophes of possession.

   Rachels books are in the box. _____

   The mens cloakrooms are there. _____

   St James School is very big. _____

   She is a childrens writer. _____

2. Rewrite each phrase to show possession.

   For example: 'The cat belonging to Simon' becomes 'Simon's cat'.

   the whiskers belonging to the cat _____

   the scarf belonging to Robert _____

   the football belonging to Jones _____

   the doors belonging to the cars _____

Common Letter Clusters

Key Words

letter cluster
accents
dialects
phonemes
homophones

↻ Recap

A **letter cluster** is a pattern of letters which appears within many words. Letter clusters can make different sounds.

🗒 Revise

Here are some common letter clusters and words which use them.

In different parts of the country, words may be pronounced differently depending on local **accents** and **dialects**. This is especially true of 'our' words.

our

flour

hour

journey

pour

sour

In our spelling system, a letter cluster can represent different **phonemes** (sounds). You can see this clearly in words featuring the 'ough' letter cluster, but this can be tricky as the same letter cluster can be used for more than one phoneme. This means that the same letter cluster can be pronounced in different ways depending on the word.

ough

cough

drought

thorough

tough

wrought

ear

bear

dreary

fear

hearth

weary

Look at the difference between 'height' and 'weight', for example. Both use the same letter cluster but they are pronounced differently.

ight

bright

eight

height

sight

weight

ice

apprentice

dice

mice

practice

twice

Look out for **homophones** which may sound the same but have different meanings and spellings.

For example, 'sought' means to seek and 'sort' means to arrange or categorise.

✔ Check

1. The words in the box all use the letter cluster 'aus'. Use one word to complete each sentence.

sausage	pause	claustrophobia	clause	cause

The main _____ in the sentence makes sense on its own.

_____ is a fear of enclosed spaces.

They had to _____ the film to answer the door.

The dog stole a _____ roll from the plate.

Human activity is the main _____ of climate change.

2. Think of words with the 'ough' letter cluster to answer the following questions.

Think of two words where the letter cluster 'ough' makes the sound 'uff'.

_____   _____

Think of two words where the letter cluster 'ough' makes the sound 'off'.

_____   _____

Think of two words where the letter cluster 'ough' makes the sound 'ow'.

_____   _____

Think of one word where the letter cluster 'ough' makes the sound 'oe' (as in 'toe').

_____

Think of a word where the letter cluster 'ough' makes the 'aw' sound.

_____

Prefixes

↺ Recap

A prefix is a letter or cluster of letters added to the beginning of a word to change its meaning or make a new word.

📄 Revise

Prefixes can change the meaning of a word, sometimes creating the opposite meaning.

For example: The prefix 'un' means 'not'.

    un + necessary = unnecessary

    un + fortunate = unfortunate

    un + made = unmade

For example: The prefix 'sub' means 'under'.

    sub + marine = submarine

    sub + way = subway

    sub + terranean = subterranean

✔ Check

> Remembering prefixes and their meanings can support your spelling and vocabulary development.

1. Draw lines to link the prefixes with their correct meaning.

bi	undo
contra	out of
de	against
in	not
pro	ahead
ex	two

2. Find three examples of words that use the following prefixes. You can use a dictionary to help you.

anti (meaning against)

_____ _____ _____

re (meaning again)

_____ _____ _____

inter (meaning between)

_____ _____ _____

mis (meaning wrong)

_____ _____ _____

non (meaning not)

_____ _____ _____

Suffixes

↺ Recap

A suffix is a letter or a cluster of letters placed at the end of a word to change its meaning or create a new word.

📄 Revise

The suffix 'al' means relating to:

    lyric + al = lyrical

    hysteric + al = hysterical

    addition + al = additional

The suffix 'est' means most:

    brave + est = bravest

    rich + est = richest

    strong + est = strongest

For vowel suffixes, if the root word ends in 'e', drop the 'e' and add the suffix.

For example: fierce = fiercest

For words ending in a consonant + y, change the 'y' to 'i' and add the vowel suffix.

For example: dry = driest and funny = funniest

✔ Check

1. Draw lines to link the suffixes with their correct meaning.

ly	full of
ful	of, resembling
less	without
ic	a person who is expert or concerned in
ist	doing or tending to do something
ive	in this manner

2. Find three examples of words that use the following suffixes. You can use a dictionary to help you.

er (meaning person/thing performing a particular action)

_____   _____   _____

ary (meaning of, belonging to)

_____   _____   _____

tion (meaning action/result of a [verb])

_____   _____   _____

Common Errors

↻ Recap

Spelling words correctly brings clarity to your writing. You can develop strategies to help you remember difficult words.

📝 Revise

Here are some commonly used spelling strategies:

- Break the word into syllables, for example, 're-mem-ber'.
- Break the word into **affixes**, for example, 'dis + appear'.
- Link with word families, for example, 'joy' = 'joyful'/'enjoyment'.
- Refer to **etymology**, for example, 'micro' means small – used in 'microscopic'/'microfilm'.
- Change the sound of the word to make it memorable, for example, 'de-FIN-ite'.
- Say letter names to a rhythmic beat, like a chant, for example, 'g-u-a-r-d'.
- Invent slogans to help you remember words, for example, 'necessary' = 'one **c**ollar two **s**ocks'.
- Find words within words, for example, '*asses*sment', 'con*science*'.
- Keep a list of words you need to learn.
- Use *look/say/cover/write/check* regularly to learn new words or highlight your errors.
- Use a dictionary.

Here is a list of high frequency words that are often misspelled. Highlight any words you find difficult to spell. Use one or more of the strategies above to help you to learn them.

actually	disappear	listening	remember
although	embarrass	lovely	safety
analyse	environment	marriage	separate
assessment	eerie	necessary	sincerely
beautiful	February	nervous	technology
beginning	fulfil	parallel	tomorrow
conscience	guard	permanent	unfortunately
conscious	interrupt	people	weight
decision	issue	queue	weird
definite	knowledge	receive	women

It is important that you check spellings in your writing and recognise your errors. Keep a list of tricky words and try different strategies to help you learn them.

✔ Check

Homophones are words that have the same pronunciation but different meanings and spellings.

1. Write a sentence using each of these commonly confused homophones.

allowed _____

aloud _____

braking _____

breaking _____

course _____

coarse _____

site _____

sight _____

source _____

sauce _____

threw _____

through _____

2. Circle the correct word.

It was to/too/two late to go to the park.

Their/There/They're going to the cinema.

I am going to offer my friend some advise/advice.

The train was stationery/stationary for 45 minutes.

Please can I borrow you're/your phone?

Glossary

A

accents – ways of pronouncing words that are distinctive to an area or country.

active voice – the subject of a sentence performs the action. For example: The cat chased the mouse. The cat is the subject.

affixes – additions to the base stems of words to create new words or modify their meaning, for example, 'appear' and 'disappear'.

alliteration – repetition of a sound or letter for impact.

anecdote – a short interesting or amusing story.

argument – reasons or ideas to support a theory.

auxiliary verbs – support another verb to suggest tense, mood or voice.

C

character – a person or key figure in a novel, play, film or poem.

colon – a punctuation mark (:) used to separate two independent clauses or to introduce a list or quotation.

complex sentence – contains one main clause and at least one subordinate clause to add information to the main clause. For example: Although it was cold, we didn't wear our coats.

compound sentence – two independent clauses joined by 'and', 'but', 'or', 'so'. For example: We wore our boots or we wore our sandals.

conjunctions – used to link ideas in a sentence or paragraph, for example, 'and', 'if', 'but'.

connecting adverbials – connect ideas and sentences to signal connections, for example, 'although', 'after'.

connectives – words or phrases that join ideas in sentences or a text.

context – background information that helps the reader to understand a text, for example, historical information, cultural information or an additional backstory of a character.

contraction – a shortened version of a word, for example, 'shouldn't' rather than 'should not'.

coordinating conjunction – used to link two independent clauses in a sentence. The three main coordinating conjunctions are 'and', 'but' and 'or'.

D

dialects – forms of language that are particular to a region or group of people.

E

emotive language – language used to evoke an emotional response in the reader.

etymology – the history of a word or phrase.

extended metaphor – a metaphor that is developed over lines or a whole text.

F

fact – something that is known or can be proved to be true.

figurative language – use of similes, metaphors, onomatopoeia, alliteration and other devices to communicate meaning or ideas.

formal register – language that is precise and professional in tone.

G

genre – a style of literature or art, for example, horror, romance, suspense.

H

homophones – words that sound the same but have different meanings and spellings; for example, knew/new.

I

independent clause – a sentence that contains a subject and a verb.

infer – make a conclusion from evidence in the text; read between the lines.

inference – the process of inferring; reaching a conclusion from evidence in the text.

informal register – a conversational use of language.

information retrieval – the ability to find specific information in a text.

information text – non-fiction writing that gives information about a particular topic.

L

line length – used by a poet to create rhythm or to place emphasis on certain words.

M

main clause – a clause that could be used as a simple sentence on its own but is part of a longer sentence.

metaphors – describe an object or person by referring to something with similar characteristics.

modal verbs – help to express possibility, permission, ability or necessity, for example, 'should go', 'must do'.

N

narrative structure – the order of the events in a story.

O

object – the person or thing that is acted on by the verb.

onomatopoeic (onomatopoeia) – sounds like the word itself, for example, buzz, bang, whisper.

opinion – a view or judgement formed about something.

oxymoron – a figure of speech that combines seemingly opposite meanings, for example, organised chaos.

P

parenthesis – the overarching term for brackets, dashes and commas that are used within sentences to add information.

passive voice – the action of the verb is done to the subject. For example: He was hit.

personification – a non-human element is described with human characteristics.

phonemes – the smallest units of sounds in a word, for example, the 'c' in cat.

poetic form – the type of poem, for example, sonnet, ballad, free verse.

possession (apostrophe) – shows who/what owns something.

possessive pronoun – used to show ownership, for example, 'his book', 'her book'.

prefix – a letter or cluster of letters placed at the start of a word to change its meaning or make a new word, for example, 'understanding'/'misunderstanding', 'logical'/'illogical'.

purpose – why a text has been written, for example, to inform, to entertain.

R

relative clause – gives more information about a noun in a sentence.

relative pronoun – introduces relative clauses, for example, 'that', 'which', 'who', 'whom' and 'whose'.

reporting clause – reports who has said something in direct speech, for example, 'she said'.

review – discusses the quality of a book, play, poem, piece of art or experience.

rhetorical devices – use of language to have an impact on the reader or audience.

rhyme scheme – ordered pattern of rhyme within a poem.

rhythm – a regular, repeated pattern of beats within literature.

rule of three – ideas, words or sentences presented in groups of three for impact.

S

scan – read rapidly to find specific facts or words.

semicolon – a punctuation mark (;) used to join two independent clauses that are similar in ideas; it can also be used in place of a comma to separate phrases in a list.

similes – comparisons using 'like' or 'as'.

simple sentence – made up of one clause, containing a subject and a verb.

speech marks – punctuation used to indicate words that are spoken in a text (direct speech).

stanza – a recurring structure of a group of lines in a poem.

structure – the arrangement of ideas in a written text or speech.

subject – the person, place or thing that is performing the action of the sentence.

subordinate clause – a clause that does not make complete sense on its own: usually introduced by a subordinate conjunction; a 'wh' pronoun; that; or an -ing or -ed verb.

subordinate/subordinating conjunction – introduces a subordinate clause, for example, 'unless', 'after'.

suffix – a letter or cluster of letters placed at the end of the word to change its meaning or create a new word, for example, 'beauty'/'beautiful', 'mercy/merciless'.

syllables – single, unbroken vowel sounds within a word, for example, 'book' = 1 syllable; analyse = 3 syllables.

T

topic sentence – the sentence which states the main idea of a paragraph.

W

writer's intention – what the writer set out to do, for example, to entertain, shock, encourage a call to action.

Answers

READING

Page 5 Retrieving Information
1. a pinch (of salt)
2. until just combined
3. 15 minutes
4. They will be golden brown and a skewer inserted into the middle of each cake will come out clean.
5. a bowl, electric whisk, something to scrape the bowl, a spoon, cupcake cases, a skewer, wire rack, baking/oven tray

Page 6 Understanding the Purpose of a Fiction Text
1. Any appropriate answer. For example: The bear whispered that it was unwise to be friends with someone who would desert him in a moment of danger.
2. Any appropriate answer. For example: Misfortune is the test of true friendship. The story shows the reader that your true friends will stand by you when there is trouble. In this fable, the man was deserted by his friend and, ironically, it was the bear who helped him by giving him some good advice.

Page 8 Understanding the Purpose of a Non-fiction Text
1. One example from: Notice and name your positive emotions; Start by simply focusing on your feelings; Pick an emotion and act to increase it.
2. One instance from: For example, you might feel proud when you answer a question right, joyful when your puppy chases you around the yard, or loved when your mom shows up at your game; You might give yourself a "Yes, I can!" pep talk before a test. Or maybe you stand up straighter and practice walking through the halls in a confident way, feeling strong and powerful.
3. One question from: What helps you feel confident? How can you get more of that feeling?
4. to instruct

Page 10 Understanding Fictional Characters
1. They are behaving frantically, while looking for the tin opener.
2. Harris tries to open the tin with a pocket-knife. He breaks the knife and cuts himself.
3. George tries to open the tin with scissors and nearly hurts his eye.
4. Jerome tries to make a hole in the tin with the boat hook and is thrown into the water.
5. Any appropriate answer. For example: Throughout the extract, the characters have been behaving in a 'mad' and angry way as they try to open the tin of pineapple. The final sentence is ironic as it suggests that only now are they going to get 'mad' and angry. The writer is laughing at the characters and expects the reader to laugh with him.

Page 12 Identifying the Main Point in Non-fiction Texts
1. to summarise the film
2. fauna or wildlife
3. Colonel Miles Quaritch, who is an autonomous avatar in Na'vi form
4. A giant whale-like creature called a tulkun
5. The following text should be highlighted:
   1. To perform in the underwater scenes, Cameron brought in world champion free diver Kirk Krack to teach the cast how to do sustained breath holds and still act.
   2. The performance-capture filming took place in a 900,000-gallon tank (built specifically for the production), which could mimic the ocean's swirling currents and crashing waves.

Page 14 Understanding Context in Fiction Texts
1. to meet again
2. upon the heath
3. before sunset
4. Shakespeare wanted to establish that supernatural and evil forces dominate the play.

Page 16 Understanding Context in Non-fiction Texts
1. being polite
2. Manners cost nothing/have helped him more in life than anything else/make other people feel more comfortable.
3. being kind

4. Sharing a smile with someone, offering to help someone with their bags or giving a compliment to someone.
5. His brother was murdered in a brutal way by people who didn't know him. He wants to highlight the need to be kind and good to each other.

Page 18 Fact or Opinion?
1.

and I don't care how many times you hear this	Example answer: opinion
it never stops being amazing	opinion
attracts more visitors every year than Greece	fact
It gets through 40 acres of potatoes a day.	fact
It has the largest concentration of roller coasters in Europe.	fact
it does what it does very well – or if not very well at least very successfully.	opinion

2. Accept an answer that says Bryson either likes or doesn't like Blackpool, as long as there are facts and opinions from the text to back up the response. For example:

   Bill Bryson likes Blackpool. For instance, he describes Blackpool as 'amazing'. He lists positive facts, for example, 'attracts more visitors every year than Greece'. He states 'it does what it does very well' and does it 'very successfully'.

   Bill Bryson dislikes Blackpool. For instance, he describes Blackpool's visitors as 'consuming more chips per capita than anywhere else in the planet'. He also points out that 'on Friday and Saturday nights it has more public toilets than anywhere else in Britain; elsewhere they call them doorways'. He also suggests that Blackpool doesn't really do things 'very well: 'it does what it does very well – or if not very well at least very successfully'.

Page 20 Inference 1
1. The songbirds 'flew backwards into the sea'. This suggests that the arrival of the Governor and the ravens is a bad thing.
2. An omen is a sign of good or bad things happening. The ravens are seen as a sign of evil.
3. The wolves and the deer ran into the sea. They knew the ravens were evil and thought this was a better fate than staying.
4. The Governor's link with the ravens suggests that he is also evil.
5. This suggests that Da feels that bad things will happen. He is worried or afraid.

Page 22 Inference 2
1. They plan to cause a scandal and turn Hyde's friends against him.
2. They were very angry: the women were 'wild as harpies'; there was a 'circle of such hateful faces'.
3. Hyde was frightened but he also showed a 'sneering coolness'.
4. Stevenson is linking Hyde with evil.
5. Hyde has no respect for the crowd/thinks he is better than them. He is calm in the face of their anger.

Page 24 Inference in Non-fiction
1. A lack of cats in the café.
2. The customer could have looked around the café for cats and talked to staff about the lack of cats.
3. The owner suggests the customer should have spoken with staff to resolve the situation.
4. Any appropriate answer. For example: defence of the cats at the café; explanation of the flea treatments the café uses for the cats; explanation of the term 'moggy' and why this doesn't apply to the cats; exploration of the range of pedigree cats at the café, for example, Maine Coon and Siamese.

Page 26 Inference and the Writer's Intention
1. 'the rays rely on electroreceptors in their skin'
2. Three examples from: 'their eyes are bad'; 'they literally inhale their food'; 'their spiracles 'work less efficiently than their gills'; 'breathing

as if through a towel'; 'it's like feeling the presence of someone hiding in a dark room'; 'special gel-filled pits'.

3. The writer adds details of how the stingray hunts using 'electroreceptors in their skin' and how the stingray eats: 'inhale their food, gulping down the electric signal'. She questions how this process would feel: 'Do they get a little light-headed…?' and uses an explanation from a YouTube video showing her research and interest.

4. The writer wants the reader to understand how the stingray is perfectly designed as a poisonous creature. Everything about the stingray, from bones, tissue and electric senses, is designed to protect itself. The writer wants the reader to feel a sense of wonder that the stingray is so magnificent.

Page 28 Identifying Themes

1.

humankind's confrontation with nature	someone struggles in a storm at sea
death	a funeral brings a family together
growing up	moving to university
love	falling in love for the first time
conflict	two friends fight over who was right and who was wrong

2. Any appropriate answers.
For example:
Friendship: how childhood friends support each other throughout their lives.
Greed: a man steals from a charity shop.
Abuse of power: A warrior kills a king.
Dreams and ambitions: A child dreams of being a human rights lawyer.
Betrayal: A prisoner of war reveals an escape plan to the guards.

3.

Struggles between generations make for a roller coaster of a plot.	family conflict
On the shores of a sleepy seaside town, something hideous crawls from the sea.	good versus evil
The village had its own ways of thinking. They had worked – until now.	change versus tradition
In this rite-of-passage novel, we learn the struggles of realising that parents don't always know best.	growing up

Page 30 Structuring an Argument

2. This states the position clearly as a three-word catchy slogan to capture the reader's interest. It is a powerful statement, suggesting that change must happen.

3. Emotive language is used like 'misled', suggesting that the gas and oil companies have lied to the public. 'Cooking our planet' adds a sense of drama to the consequences of the companies' actions. This is further emphasised by the violence of 'murderous floods, deadly droughts and rainforests on fire'.

4. The emotive language used suggests that the campaign group do not trust the actions of the 'top' CEOs. They accuse them of 'pretending', which plays on our emotions of betrayal and suggests that we should not trust them. 'Billions in profit' suggests that the companies only care about money. The text also highlights the contradictions of actions – they attend a climate conference yet continue to pursue profits.

5. The group is stating their plan. 'Demanding' is emotive as it suggests that action must happen. It is a call for united action – 'millions of us' to stand together against these companies.

Page 32 Language Choices in Fiction

1. • Single-sentence paragraphs: 'Then it was gone.'; 'And Stanley wasn't sure whether he'd seen it or not.'
   • Contrasting sentence lengths: 'The humidity, or maybe the electricity in the air, had made Zigzag's hair even more wild-looking.

His frizzy blonde hair stuck almost straight out'; 'Stanley could count more than thirty seconds between the flash of lightning and the clap of thunder. That was how far away the storm was.'
   • Repetition of words or the rule of three: 'Two rattlesnakes. Two scorpions. Two yellow-spotted lizards.'

2. Three examples from: 'A storm was way off to the west, beyond the mountains. Stanley could count more than thirty seconds between the flash of lightning and the clap of thunder.'; 'Sound travels a great distance…'; 'Usually, Stanley couldn't see the mountains at this time of day.'; '… every time the lightning flashed, the dark shape of the mountains would briefly appear.'; '"C'mon, rain!" shouted Armpit'; '"Maybe it'll rain so hard it will fill up the whole lake"'; 'The horizon lit up with a huge web of lightning'.

3. The answer could outline how Sachar:
   • uses senses of hearing and sight to describe the storm
   • shows that this is an unusual and intimidating event by telling us what Stanley can usually see
   • shows the boys speculating about what could happen
   • describes physical changes to Zigzag's hair because of the storm
   • shows the movement of the storm
   • uses dramatic images of the mountain as it is lit up by lightning.

Page 34 Language Choices in Poetry

1.

'And both that morning equally lay/In leaves no step had trodden black'	The paths are equally covered in leaves so the speaker can't follow anyone's route or ask for advice.
'Oh, I kept the first for another day!'	The speaker thinks that they will return and perhaps take the first path one day.
'Yet knowing how way leads on to way/I doubted if I should ever come back.'	The speaker knows that once choices are made it is hard to go back.
'I shall be telling this with a sigh/Somewhere ages and ages hence:'	The speaker knows that they may regret this choice in later life.

2. The speaker took the 'less travelled' path – the more unusual path. This choice 'made all the difference' perhaps positively or perhaps negatively.

Page 36 Language Choices in Non-fiction

1. balcony appearance at Buckingham Palace; UK-wide light show; a concert; a solemn religious service.

2. Saturday, May 6 to Monday, May 8.

3. What happened?

4. The concert was broadcast live featuring global and contemporary stars. Several thousand members of the public received free tickets. There was an orchestra, entertainers and dancers. A Coronation Choir of amateur singers took part.

Page 38 Figurative and Poetic Language

1. The merlin has 'fast, powerful wing beats', then 'short, precise glides' while it is looking for prey. A buzzard glides and a kestrel hovers.

As a rule	conversational language as if chatting with the reader
It (and many other species, too) can detect ultraviolet light, invisible to the naked human eye	contrast to illustrate the differences between the bird and human abilities
A kestrel can spot a dor beetle 50 metres away.	direct language to give factual information to the reader
Exploding from their lookout post,	metaphor shows the powerful burst of the bird's movement
Handy, if a vole is their snack of choice!	lighthearted comment emphasising the purposeful nature of the bird

Answers

Page 40 Structure in Poetry

1. The poem is about an eagle in the wild.
2. Stanza 1: The eagle is holding onto the crag (the rock). He is standing still against the sky.
   Stanza 2: The eagle watches, then plunges in pursuit of his prey.
3. The rhyme scheme is tight and controlled using only one rhyme in each stanza. This reflects the power of the eagle as he moves from watcher to fierce hunter.
   This statement outlines the rhyme scheme and explains what it tells the reader about the eagle.
4. a. The contrast is from stillness to sudden movement.
   b. Throughout the poem, Tennyson emphasises the eagle's power through his stillness and control. He 'clasps' the crag, 'he stands' and surveys his environment. The final movement is sudden and unexpected – just like a thunderbolt would be, showing that the eagle is powerful, controlled and deadly.

Page 42 Structure in Non-fiction

1. A vegan dog diet – does it exist?
2. 1. A vegan diet does exist but is hard to get right.
   2. Dogs should eat meat unless advised by a vet.
   3. Contact a vet before using vegan diets; otherwise you could put your dog at risk.
   4. Vegan diets for dogs can be expensive and difficult to follow.
   5. Dogs should only become vegans as a last resort.

Page 44 Rhetorical Devices in Non-fiction

1.

Use of figures to support ideas/ argument	With today's emissions levels, that remaining CO_2 budget will be entirely gone within less than 8.5 years.
Suggestion of group involvement by using 'us'/'we'	One example from: Your generation is failing us. And if you choose to fail us, I say we will never forgive you. We will not let you get away with this. Right here, right now is where we draw the line.
Issue of a warning – change now or this will happen	The eyes of all future generations are upon you. And if you choose to fail us, I say we will never forgive you.
Use of a three-part list for emphasis	We will not let you get away with this. Right here, right now is where we draw the line. The world is waking up.

2. The tone of the speech is angry and determined. The use of emotive language supports this.

Page 46 Figurative Devices in Fiction

1. a. being alone
   b. sealed away from its environment
   c. He was sealed away from all people who could love and care for him and people he could love.
2. a. Hard and sharp as flint
   b. It suggests Scrooge was cold and spiky towards people.
3. a. personification
   b. The house was young and playful before Scrooge moved in. It wasn't always dreary.
   c. Scrooge has driven all the love and fun from the house. It is now as dreary and cold as he is. Other acceptable answer is that it suggests that Scrooge is also lonely/isolated.

WRITING

Page 48 Personal Letters

1. Any appropriate paragraph. For example: I heard that you have been offered the opportunity to study abroad and I think you should seize it!

2.

Notes	P2	P3
I know you will miss your friends but we can video call as often as you want.		✓
What a great opportunity this is!	✓	
It might seem that it's a long way away, but flights are available and are easy to work out.		✓
There will be so many new foods to try and new sights to see.	✓	
Imagine being fluent in another language!	✓	
It is only two years. Time will fly.		✓

3. Any appropriate paragraph. For example: This sounds like a really great opportunity. Good luck and I will see you soon.

Page 50 Formal Letters

1. Any appropriate paragraph. For example: I would like to apply for the Saturday job that was advertised in your shop.

2.

Notes	P2	P3
I am a reliable worker and know that you could rely on me in this role.	✓	
My participation in school sports teams which means that I am a team player and know how to work alongside others.		✓
I am calm under pressure and can make decisions quickly when I need to.	✓	
I have had a paper round for the past year and have learned how to manage my time effectively.		✓
I like working as part of a team and enjoy meeting new people.	✓	
I am a member of the school council and am used to talking with adults in a range of situations.		✓

3. Any appropriate paragraph. For example: Thank you for your time and I look forward to discussing the job in an interview.

Page 52 Writing Articles

1.

Notes	P1	P2	P3
Everyone is nervous on the first day.	✓		
Make sure you have equipment for the day, such as a pen, reading book.			✓
You will be given a map to help you navigate the school.		✓	
Everyone has had a first day at the school – even the teachers.	✓		
Make your packed lunch or snack the night before.			✓
Is your uniform labelled with your name? Schools have lots of students and things often get lost.			✓
Your tutor will give you a copy of your timetable – don't lose it!		✓	
You will be tired after your first day – get an early night!			✓
Practise your journey to school.			✓
There will be systems in place to help and support you.		✓	
Teachers will explain what happens in class and what you can expect from each subject.		✓	
Everyone gets lost!	✓		

2. Any appropriate article, using the notes outlined in the Check.

Success criteria:

The student should check their draft and consider these questions:

- Did you make a plan?
- Have you thought about audience and purpose?
- Have you included the headline?
- Does your opening paragraph give an overview of the subject?
- Have you used all the interesting facts from the notes to inform and reassure pupils?

An appropriate headline for the article could be: 'Don't panic!' or 'Everyone's on your side'

Page 54 Speeches

1. Any appropriate paragraph. For example: Good afternoon everyone. I am here today to put forward my ideas about curriculum time for PE.

2. Across 5–15-year-olds, 8.1.6% do sport. 77.8% take part in school and 37.9% take part outside school.

3. Any three benefits from the following, or any other appropriate answers:

Teaches the importance of rules and discipline

Works off excess energy

Helps with social and team working skills

Improves self-esteem

4. Your speech should follow this structure:

Paragraph 1: Address the audience

Paragraph 2: Briefly say what you will be talking about

Paragraph 3: Outline why this topic is important to you

Paragraph 4: Outline what will happen if nothing is done about your topic

Paragraph 5: Sign off, directly addressing the audience

Success criteria:

The student should check their draft and consider these questions:

- Did you make a plan?
- Have you thought about audience and purpose?
- Does your second paragraph give an overview of the subject?
- Have you used facts and statistics to support your argument?
- Have you signed off your speech effectively?

Page 56 Planning a Narrative

This is the plot of William Shakespeare's *Romeo and Juliet*.

Page 57

1.

Normality	A warrior wins a battle and is given titles and lands by the king.
Disruption/problem	The warrior is given a prophecy that he will become king one day. With his wife he decides to kill the king so that the prophecy will become true.
Climax	The warrior kills the king and takes over as the new king.
Search for resolution	The warrior king begins to feel insecure in his position and commits terrible murders to keep his power. The nobles turn against him.
Return to normality/ new normal	The nobles kill the warrior king and put another king in his place.

2. Any appropriate answer. For example:

Normality	A girl had left school without her best friend, as she needed to get to football. It was an important match.
Disruption/ problem	Around the corner, the terrifying bullies who play for the rival football team were waiting and she was alone.
Climax	The bully group began taunting and making fun of the girl. They knew that she needed to concentrate for the match and set out to destroy her confidence.
Search for resolution	The girl's best friend, who had heard that the bullies were waiting, came around the corner. She stepped in to protect the girl. The girl stood up for herself.
Return to normality/ new normal	The girl's team won the match and the friends walked home together.

Page 58 Planning a Description

1. Any appropriate answer. For example:

Part 1: overview of the scene Where/what is it? What is the mood/atmosphere?	A bustling busy market. Shoppers are talking to each other and carrying bags full of purchases.
Part 2: zoom in to details What are the key colours? What catches your eye first?	Red and green are key colours of the fruits on the stall. Pink and gold details in the fabrics on the stalls and the vehicles. The eye is drawn to the sumptuous mound of ripe apples.
Part 3: contrasts What contrasting moods/atmospheres can you see/imagine? What contrasts can you find?	Light is fading and the stalls are being packed away. Tables and awnings are being packed into vans and lorries. Noises: metal clanging as stalls and tables are packed away. Sounds of people clearing and sweeping the space.
Part 4: ending How will you end your description? Will you zoom into a small detail? Will you use a contrast?	The stalls have closed. The market is now completely clear of the stalls. The people, both stall holders and customers, have gone home. Sense of rest, ready for the next day.

2. Success criteria

The student should check their draft and consider these questions:

- Have you used the descriptive writing structure to shape your description?
- Have you used the plan to structure your writing?
- Have you included an overview of the scene?
- Have you zoomed into details?
- Have you included contrasts?
- Have you considered how to end your writing?

Page 60 Formal and Informal Register

1. Informal: What d'ya mean?; I'm not going.; I've never had a proper job.

Formal I am writing to complain…; The palace was dark.; It has been announced that…

2. I have not eaten anything.

I am pleased you are here.

Please pass that hooded top.

Would you like to play football?

That was painful.

3. Any appropriate answer; Standard English/formal register should be used.

For example: At twelve thirty, I saw a group of students running across the playground. I saw one of the students fall to the ground and cry out in pain.

Answers

GRAMMAR

Page 62 Sentence Structures
1. simple sentence
2. complex sentence
3. compound sentence
4. compound sentence
5. complex sentence

Page 63 Sentence Types
1.
Today is Monday.	statement
Is it Monday today?	question
That hurt!	exclamation
Go home now.	command
Stop talking.	command
What a shame!	exclamation
The house was blue.	statement
It is raining.	statement
Stop what you are doing.	command
What day is it?	question

2. Where are we going?
3. Go to the back of the classroom.
4. Exeter is a university city.
5. That's a shame!

Page 64 Complex Sentences
1. Any appropriate answers that make sense. Below is one possible set of responses.

Subordinate clause	Main clause
Running through the mist	the rescuers managed to reach him
Growling with menace	the dogs raced into the courtyard
Shrouded in a thin white veil	the woman vanished
Etched into the edge of the window frame	the carvings were grotesque
Encouraged by her words	the fiend managed to escape
Falling through the air	the girl's life appeared before her
Tortured by memories of last night	he slunk along the corridor
Peering into the darkness	the boy called into the night
Fighting a way through the crowd	they could identify nothing

2. Any appropriate answer. For example: The dogs, growling with menace, raced into the courtyard.
3. Any appropriate answers. For example:
   The sun was hot overhead before noon.
   Although it was raining, we didn't wear our coats.
   The dogs ran towards us whenever we moved.

Page 66 Relative Clauses
1. who
2. which/that
3. that/which
4. whose
5. that/which
6. Any appropriate answer. For example: where I went until I was 11.
7. Any appropriate answer. For example: which was part of the school
8. Any appropriate answer. For example: When I get up
9. Any appropriate answer. For example: The cat, which had to be rescued from the roof, appeared in the local newspaper.
10. Any appropriate answer. For example: The orange jumper that my brother knitted fell into the sea.

Page 68 Using Modal Verbs
1. High level of certainty: will, must, should, can, shall, have to, need to
   Low level of certainty: may, might, ought to, could, would
2. I will do my homework this evening.

Page 69 Using the Active and Passive Voice
1. A top chef cooked the meal.
2. [Name/pronoun] broke the window.
3. The dog bit the man.
4. [Name/pronoun] ate the cakes.

Page 70 Connecting Ideas
1. Time: until, when, lastly, afterwards, whenever
   Contrast: alternatively, on the one hand, but, although,
   Cause and effect: as a result, because, so that
2. Any appropriate answer. For example:
   There are great concerns about the environment. **However**, no one seems to be willing to change what they do in their everyday lives.
   In spite of the fact that almost everything that supermarkets sell is covered in plastic, supermarkets do not take responsibility for collecting or recycling the plastic they have sold.
   We are strangling our planet with plastic. **For example**, plastic bags litter the countryside.

PUNCTUATION

Page 72 Direct Speech
1. "I am cold," said Kassim.
   Tamsin replied, "Would you like to borrow my jumper?"
2. Here is one possible answer:
   Knock knock.
   "Who's there?" said Kassim.
   "Lettuce," replied Tamsin.
   "Lettuce who?" questioned Kassim.
   "Let us in; it's cold out here!" laughed Tamsin.
3. "And did you really have the three wishes granted?" asked Mrs. White.
   "I did," said the Sergeant-Major, and his glass tapped against his strong teeth.
   "And has anybody else wished?" continued the old lady.
4. Any appropriate answer. For example:
   "I'm going to the park after school," said Robin. "Would you like to come too?"
   "Really sorry," said Pablo. "I have to go straight home for my tea."

   "I'm going to the park after school. Would you like to come too?" said Robin.
   "I'm really sorry but I have to go to my swimming lesson," said Pablo.

Page 74 Colons
1. I needed only three cards to win: the seven of diamonds, the ace of hearts and the queen of spades.
2. My parents had set a new rule: do your homework before using the computer.
3. The new school timetable had serious drawbacks: students had no time to eat lunch and staff had too much marking to do.
4. Elephant (noun): a large grey mammal

Page 75 Semicolons
1. She went to the library and collected: a copy of *Dune*, the next in her favourite series; an audiobook of *An Inspector Calls* and a handy revision guide.
2. The new James Bond film is showing on Wednesday 9 May at 17:30 on Thursday 10 May at 18:30; on Friday 11 May at 12:00 and 18:30 and on Saturday 12 May at 12:00.

Page 76 Parenthesis
1. The dog <u>the noisy one</u> needs to go for a walk.

2. I went <u>very reluctantly</u> for a walk.
3. The football pitch <u>owned by the club</u> was icy.

Any appropriate answers. For example:
4. – from BTS –
5. – the modern one –
6. – powerful and dangerous –
7. The class, whose parents were attending, stood proudly.
8. The boy, who was 14, represented Wales.
9. The blanket, which was green, rolled off the bed.
10. Harry Kane, whom he had admired since he was young, played for his favourite club.

Page 78 Apostrophes of Contraction
1. wasn't
   there's
   they're
   she'd
   o'clock
2. Tell me if it's too much.
   When's it time for its injection?
   It's close to the end of the film.
   John's unsure if it's correct.
   She shouldn't have done that.
   He hadn't had his dinner yet.
   The dog wouldn't have barked.

Page 79 Apostrophes of Possession
1. Rachel's books are in the box.
   The men's cloakrooms are there.
   St James's School is very big.
   She is a children's writer.
   He is the boys' teacher.
   The spider was huge and its legs, long.
2. the cat's whiskers
   Robert's scarf
   Jones' football
   the cars' doors

SPELLING

Page 80 Common Letter Clusters
1. clause
   claustrophobia
   pause
   sausage
   cause
2. Any appropriate answers. For example:
   tough; rough
   cough; trough
   plough; drought
   though
   dough; though
   sought; brought

Page 82 Prefixes
1.
bi	two
contra	against
de	undo
in	not
pro	ahead
ex	out of

2. Any appropriate answers. For example:
   antiseptic; antibiotics; antidote

react; remember; report
international; intercity; interact
mistake; mislead; misfit
nonsense; non-stick; non-conformist

Page 83 Suffixes
1.
ly	in this manner
ful	full of
less	without
ic	doing or tending to do something
ist	a person who is expert or concerned in
ive	of, resembling

2. Any appropriate answers. For example:
   performer; singer; driver
   secondary; sedentary; ancillary
   revolution; commendation; starvation

Page 84 Common Errors
1. Any appropriate answers. For example:
   I'm not allowed to go.
   She spoke aloud.
   The car was braking.
   Her bag was breaking.
   My GCSE course is good.
   Coarse fabric rubbed his feet.
   This is the site of the archaeological dig.
   The book was in plain sight.
   This is the source of the river.
   I love cheese sauce.
   She threw the keys.
   He walked through the door.
2. too
   They're
   advice
   stationary
   your

Progress Tracker

Reading	Revised	Checked
Retrieving Information		
Understanding the Purpose of a Fiction Text		
Understanding the Purpose of a Non-fiction Text		
Understanding Fictional Characters		
Identifying the Main Point in Non-fiction Texts		
Understanding Context in Fiction Texts		
Understanding Context in Non-fiction Texts		
Fact or Fiction?		
Inference 1		
Inference 2		
Inference in Non-fiction		

Reading	Revised	Checked
Inference and the Writer's Intention		
Identifying Themes		
Structuring an Argument		
Language Choices in Fiction		
Language Choices in Poetry		
Language Choices in Non-fiction		
Figurative and Poetic Language		
Structure in Poetry		
Structure in Non-fiction		
Rhetorical Devices in Non-fiction		
Figurative Devices in Fiction		

Writing	Revised	Checked
Personal Letters		
Formal Letters		
Writing Articles		
Speeches		
Planning a Narrative		
Planning a Description		
Formal and Informal Register		

Grammar	Revised	Checked
Sentence Structures		
Sentence Types		
Complex Sentences		
Relative Clauses		
Using Modal Verbs		
Using the Active and Passive Voice		
Connecting Ideas		

Punctuation	Revised	Checked
Direct Speech		
Colons		
Semicolons		
Parenthesis		
Apostrophes of Contraction		
Apostrophes of Possession		

Spelling	Revised	Checked
Common Letter Clusters		
Prefixes		
Suffixes		
Common Errors		

Notes